AN UNBELIEVABLE JOURNEY
FROM GED TO CEO

THE MOST
UNLIKELY
LEADER

ROGER SMITH

Ballast Books, LLC
Washington, DC
www.ballastbooks.com

ISBN: 978-1-955026-13-0

Library of Congress Control Number has been applied for

Printed in Canada

Published by Ballast Books
www.ballastbooks.com

For more information, bulk orders, appearances or speaking requests,
please email info@ballastbooks.com

TABLE OF CONTENTS

PART III: CLEAN AT LAST

PART IV: AT THE HELM

INTRODUCTION

Which rock bottom should I begin with? This was the question I pondered as I started to piece together my life story for this memoir. Do I begin with leaving my mom's house at age fifteen with no place to live? Or with the living room in a Sunset Strip massage parlor that I called home as a sixteen-year-old? Maybe I should start with thumbing my way up and down the coast of California with no job or money or place to be.

I could begin like a movie with a scene of me as a fifteen-year-old, hanging out in a Santa Monica pool hall, and going from sniffing a glue-like solvent called toluene to shooting heroin within a year. Or perhaps I could start a few years later, when I got married and then quickly divorced as a teenager? That's a compelling place to start, except that wasn't exactly rock bottom; that was more like a weigh station on the way to rock bottom.

In fact, if there were a deadbeat to-do list of things to accomplish to reach rock bottom, I put a big fat check mark next to all of them.

I was kicked out of high school multiple times and never graduated.

I was arrested as a kid more times than I can count.

I was a drug addict.

I was hospitalized.

I was homeless.

I stole.

My best friend was shot right next to me while pulling a robbery.

Even as I write this I can't believe my life turned out as it did. There was almost nothing I can point to in my first twenty years on this earth that would indicate that I'd get my shit together at some point and be competent enough to hold a job, keep a job, and eventually run anything—let alone an entire company or two or three.

But that's the ending of my story. If you're reading this, then you have an idea of how things turned out. What you don't know is how improbable my career and my journey through life have been. That's the reason I was drawn to start this book with one of my many rock bottoms. I have an innate desire to let you know how far I've come. Maybe it stems from a latent need to prove myself because I thought I'd never amount to anything. Maybe it's just ego. Or maybe it's an excuse to put it all on paper for posterity so I know that it really happened this way. It's probably a mixture of all three, and I'm sure a psychologist could come up with a whole buffet of other reasons.

One thing I know for sure is that I want to share my story to tell you that your life and your career and who you are as a person are all within your hands. You can fall all the way down to a dark place where you can't see your way out...and then through sheer grit and gumption and tenacity (and yeah, a little luck in the right places and a lot of blessings), you can claw your way out.

Because that's what I did.

So you know what?

Here's the truth:

The reason I can't decide which rock bottom to start with is because I had so damn many of them. And it doesn't matter which one I open with (divorces, drugs, rehab, relapses, running away—take your pick) because, frankly, they're all dark as hell, and looking back I can't believe that all of them happened to one guy—me. Instead, what I'm going to do is start at the beginning, at the earliest memories of my childhood, and then we'll go through the highs (literally and figuratively) and the lows and everything in between together.

Buckle up.

PART I

A VAGABOND CHILDHOOD

CHAPTER 1

New York City, 1958

My mother grew up in the Bronx in New York City, and I was born in Queens. I was two years old when my dad went to prison and my mom became the breadwinner of the house. I don't remember much about my biological father, and frankly, I don't have much to say about him. What I do know is that he and my mother married when she was very young, and after he went to jail, she took all kinds of jobs to keep us afloat; really, anything to make a buck.

When I was a little kid, we lived in a small two-bedroom apartment in Queens that practically backed up to my elementary school, PS 139. My mom had her own room, and I shared a room with my two siblings: my sister Tina, who was four years older than me, and my brother Bob, who was two years older. One of my mother's jobs at this time was working in sales for a fashion company

5

called Feathercombs. After she started working there she got involved with the CEO, Andy Smith.

Andy and my mom dated for a long time, and somewhere around the time I was in second grade they married—and that's where I got my last name. Andy's business was very successful, and we moved out of the apartment in Queens into an incredible three-story brownstone building on 92nd street on the east side of Manhattan between Madison Avenue and 5th. This place was really fancy. We had a big outside garden, there was a giant spiral staircase that went from the first to the second floor, and we even had a dumbwaiter. It was like a big playground for us, and the location was perfect—we were about one block east of Central Park and two blocks north of the Guggenheim Museum. I didn't know it at the time, but this was the closest I'd get to living the high life for decades.

For a brief period of time the family seemed to be on solid footing. There was an adult male in the house, parents at home, money (a little) in the bank, and from the outside we looked to be a normal family. We weren't the Cleavers or anything like that, but we at least had the aura of being functional.

We even got to travel a bit because of Andy's job. We spent some time in Quebec, Canada and a month or so in

Nice, France, and in my little brain, this was it! We had it made and things would be this way forever.

I was too young to be aware of it at the time, but Andy's business became embroiled in a copyright lawsuit with Revlon and, much to our demise, Revlon won the case and our fortunes changed forever. While Andy tried to save his business and my mom tried to help out by taking some modeling jobs, my brother and sister and I were often left alone to our own devices.

Although I was young, I knew we didn't have a real family-type environment. This wasn't the kind of house where we all came home from school, sat down at our desks and did our homework, and then went off to tee ball or ballet or piano lessons. Ha! Not close.

There was a lady named Alma who took care of us, but we were mostly unsupervised, and we fought—a lot. Looking back on it, I'm uncomfortable with how much we physically fought as kids. I can't imagine allowing my kids to do that, but there was nobody there to stop us. With my mother often away, it was up to my older sister to take on the role of "mom" when she could.

By the time I was eight years old I had a pretty good sense that it was going to be entirely up to me to carve my own path toward whatever I was going to become in the world. I knew that my mom was out in the world trying to make money any way she could, so my third-grade brain latched on to that idea.

How does a little kid make money on the Upper East Side of Manhattan in 1958?

Easy.

He takes to the streets of New York City—solo—in his jeans and his little button-down shirts and he sells stuff.

Of course, I didn't have anything of my own to sell, so I solved that problem by stealing my brother's stuff—specifically, his comic books.

My business plan was simple: Grab whatever Superman or Batman or Green Lantern comic books my brother had lying around, hide them in my shirt, and sneak out of the house. I'd walk a few blocks west to the East 96th Street Playground and then make my way through Central Park, hawking Batman versus the Joker or Superman comics for a nickel an issue. But it wasn't as if Bob had an endless supply of comics for me to sell. When the comics supply ran out, I'd wander through the park and ask people if they wanted me to walk their dog for them. I loved dogs. I loved all animals (and still do).

One of the strongest memories of my childhood is bringing stray animals back to our brownstone. Dogs. Cats. The occasional injured bird. I had a soft spot for them and I'd try to save them. There was no money in taking a stray puppy off the street, but I did scrounge up a few bucks by walking other people's dogs. I'd charge a dollar for a half-hour walk. I'd even hang around the other brownstones on my street and offer my dog-walking services. Work ethic, as you can see, was never something I lacked.

Supervision, however, was a totally different story.

Left to my own devices, I'd wander the city, stealing small candies and comics from the pharmacies and convenience stores that lined the Upper East Side all the way to Harlem. Some days I'd take the subway south to midtown or kill some time near the Metropolitan Museum of Art and then work my way over to Rockefeller Center or Broadway.

Keep in mind, this wasn't the modern-day New York City where these areas of Manhattan are now glorified shopping malls and tourist spots. Hell, no. This was New York City in the late 1950s. The city was rampant with drugs, murders, prostitution, homelessness, and every vice you can think of. Everyone chain-smoked. Everyone acted like assholes.

Those are the images I have of the city growing up. I'd walk down the streets and, from my waist-high perspective, watch all the adults puff on cigarettes and argue and weave between cars and buses and taxis. I'd absorb the police sirens and delivery truck horns and squealing car brakes—

that was the soundtrack to my earliest years. Believe me, I understand that the idea of a first-grader strolling the Big Apple by himself seems ludicrous now (and looking back on it, still feels strange) but that's just how it was. I used to play the trombone and I'd walk from the East Side to the West Side and back, and sometimes my trombone was stolen, or I'd get mugged for the few quarters or odd dollar I might have on me. I suppose I was afraid since I was eight years old, but I don't remember ever being nervous to be on my own. I didn't know any different.

In 1961 Andy's business went bankrupt and we were forced to leave our brownstone and move into the Olcott Hotel on the other side of Central Park. The Olcott was a hotel/condo complex on 72nd Street between Columbus and Central Park West. It was a step down in size and stature (if you can call our brownstone a symbol of stature) but it was still close enough for me to skip on over to the park and continue my business as a child street hustler.

We lasted in the Olcott for only about a year, and the whole experience is a blur buried in the depths of my childhood mind. The one memory I do still have is of Andy and me dragging a schlock, pink Christmas tree through the lobby up to our place. It's funny the memories we hold on to. I don't recall any family meals or trips to Yankee Stadium or nights when we stayed in and played Monopoly or created an inside joke between us. I don't recall much warmth at all, to be honest. But I vividly remember the stares we got from the people outside the hotel and the onlookers in the lobby as my stepdad and I hauled that flamingo-colored, art deco-inspired tree through the Olcott.

That was our only Christmas in that building and my last in New York City. Shortly after the new year, Andy loaded what little possessions we had into a station wagon, and we did what everyone else did at that time when things went belly up: We headed west.

In those days, if you were on the East Coast, California was like a new frontier. It felt new and exciting and it had an aura of wonderful possibilities. There was the ocean and great weather and Hollywood and new businesses, and you believed that you could make your fortune there.

That's what Andy and my mom believed, anyway.

So we packed as many of our belongings as we could into the car (including a cat and two love birds) and we moved to Malibu for a supposed "fresh start" that became anything but.

CHAPTER 2

Malibu, 1962

The picture of Malibu, California that you might have in your head is decidedly NOT the Malibu, California we moved to in the early 1960s. Where we lived there were no million-dollar mansions or giant palaces dug into the canyon. There were no celebrities ducking into Starbucks. No Lamborghinis and Range Rovers and Audis packed in traffic along the Pacific Coast Highway, inching toward 4,000-square-foot homes with panoramic views of the Pacific.

Not even close.

Back then the two-lane highway heading up the coast was loaded with beat-up Volkswagen Beetles, Dodge Darts, and Mercury Meteors, with the occasional Chevy Corvette and Ford Mustang GT, or even better, Ford Thunderbird, sprinkled in. And the road wasn't dotted with esteemed restaurants like Nobu or with gastropubs or trendy sushi joints like it is now. There were diners and some burger places and a few dive bars and restaurants for locals, but that was it.

The Malibu of my youth was a surfer town full of hippies and beach bums living in bungalows and tiny apartments and shacks. I should know, because in a very short period of time we moved in and out of about ten different places in town. We'd rent a spot for a month or two and then move on. Why? Financial reasons for one and family reasons for two.

Shortly after arriving in Malibu, my stepfather Andy found himself in the midst of a self-destructive downward spiral. I should mention here that I truly believe my stepfather had many redeeming qualities; he was an out-of-the-box thinker, and he was highly intelligent. He was also compassionate and in tune with the social injustices going on in the world at the time. My mother was that way as well, and when times were good, that was one of the things they bonded over. They had a shared view of the world and the United States, and how the racial injustices and inequality issues of the day needed to be fixed or we were headed for some bad times as a country. They were right about that. The Vietnam War and civil rights protests and demonstrations were right around the corner.

But sharing a political viewpoint wasn't enough to sustain a relationship or even a calm household. Andy was a loving person but he was his own worst enemy. While he was driving a taxi to earn money, his lifelong back problems flared up and he started taking painkillers and Valium, which really put him in a bad place mentally. He suffered. Our family suffered. During those early years in Malibu our household was very volatile. My mother left Andy and they divorced within a few years of arriving in California. That was why we moved so often—my mother was on her own and we couldn't afford the rent. She sold computer dating services before there were real computers, she sold photography sessions, and she even sold pregnant women's urine as part of some really bizarre diet fad in the early '60s. She did whatever she could to keep us afloat.

One month we'd be in a bungalow near the beach and the next month we'd be in a cottage off the highway, and then we might be in a small apartment at the base of the canyon, and on and on this went for years. The typical setup was a two-bedroom place, and all of the kids would have one room, my mother would have the other room, and there was usually a tiny kitchen or living space. As my sister got into her teenage years, my mother would give the boys one bedroom and my sister the other room for privacy, and she'd sleep in the living room.

As we moved from place to place, Andy remained somewhat involved in our lives, and whenever we got a new address he'd move somewhere down the street to be near us. There were a few times when I got older that he helped me out with personal situations, but he and my mother never reconciled. Nevertheless, Andy was there for a critical period of my life, and although I was witness to his slow, tragic slide, I vowed that even if I picked up some bad habits I would always pick myself up.

We lived in Malibu from the time I was in fifth grade until ninth grade, and it was a wonderful place to grow up and run free. Far from the intimidating and claustrophobic concrete jungle that was Manhattan, Malibu offered me and my brother and my friends a safe place to be outside and enjoy an overall healthier and more active life.

I was on the beach every single day, and as you might expect of a pre-teen living in one of the surf capitals of the world, I was bitten by the surfing bug fairly quickly. I learned to read the waves and figure out the swells and local breaks. I soaked up the beach life like a sponge. Just as trudging through Central Park as an eight-year-old was my old normal, my new normal consisted of school during the day and then off to the beach to surf or dive for abalone, or to boogie board or body board—anything in the water. It was a bare-bones lifestyle of bathing suits, hair that seemed to be permanently damp from ocean water, and saltwater-caked T-shirts (if we bothered wearing one). We had callused feet from wearing no shoes, and sunburned noses and shoulders from full days out in the surf with no sunscreen.

On days when we didn't surf, we might hike up the trails of Malibu Canyon to the waterway and then raft down, or hit Topanga Canyon and do the same thing. My life was the proverbial endless summer. It was a time when Steppenwolf's *Born to Be Wild* could be heard blasting out of teenagers' car radios and Simon & Garfunkel's *Mrs. Robinson* blared from vinyl records at my friends' houses. The Beatles released *Hey Jude* and The Doors released *Hello, I Love You*. Aretha Franklin's *Say a Little Prayer* seemed to be everywhere. I loved Jimi Hendrix and Janis Joplin because they spoke to me. The whole movement did. The peace and love stuff might seem hokey now, but back then it meant something. When I'd go to concerts or listen to those albums with my friends I felt like I was part of a community—a community I wanted to help build and promote. I loved the *feel* of it all. I loved what it all meant. I was all in on the activism and the message and the culture and the sunshine, and I never wanted it to end.

But of course, it had to.

While I was paying more attention to the incoming

surf swells and my adolescent hormones were waking up and drawing my attention to the fact that I was surrounded by attractive girls in bikinis, my mother was trying to work and provide for us. My siblings were getting older, and everyone but me seemed to need more than what our lifestyle in Malibu was providing.

Right around my freshman year of high school, we moved to the first of many places in Santa Monica and, in effect, my age of innocence was over. The period of my life that I spent in Malibu was the last time that I would be carefree, drug-free, trouble-free, and truly happy for a very long time.

CHAPTER 3

Santa Monica, 1967

Our family's move to Santa Monica improved everyone's life except mine. I'm not being melodramatic or trying to score pity points; it's just the truth. Yes, I was the youngest and I was living the life of an easygoing surf rat, but the plan to move was based on the needs of everyone else in the household (as they should have been, by the way).

My mother had a soul-crushing commute every day along the thin highways of Malibu into Santa Monica, so the move saved her time, money, and I'm sure a little sanity. My brother was enrolled at Santa Monica High School, so living in town made it easier for him to get to school and be near his friends. And my sister Tina had just enrolled at UCLA in Westwood, so having all of us nearby was good for her.

As for me, I was no longer a Malibu kid bouncing between the beach and junior high and cruising up and down the canyon. I was now closer to the West Los Angeles scene, and was a part of Los Angeles County and a more traditional city than before. There were more houses and neighborhoods and stores and bars and cops—and far more opportunity to get in trouble.

Our first place in Santa Monica was on 21st Street one block north of Wilshire. It was an area called Mid-City, and we were about a half-mile from Brentwood and what was officially West LA. With my sister off to college, my brother in high school, and my mother working, I had absolutely zero supervision. None.

By eight o'clock in the morning everyone was off to their job or school, and I had nobody to tell me that I had to do anything. I was fourteen and should have been a freshman in high school, but instead I began hanging out at a pool hall. And rather than begin my formal education on the way to college, I undertook a self-destructive DIY course on drugs, stealing, living on the street, and getting arrested an unthinkable number of times for petty crimes and misdemeanors.

This was the beginning of a period of my life when I was mostly high and made years upon years of terrible decisions. Looking back, it's a true wonder that I survived mentally intact.

The guys I hung out with at the pool hall were roughly

my age and also were from unsupervised homes and dysfunctional families. Every day we'd wake up, head to the
pool hall, and plot ways to hustle up some money so we
could buy enough drugs to keep us high through the night.
I can still picture the pool hall to this day: crappy lighting
with dark shadows throughout the room that made lunch-
time look like it could have been the middle of the night.
There was a small seating area in front, and a shitty kitchen
that served shitty food. It smelled of stale cigarettes and
weed and spilled beer and cheap cigars.

The felt on the pool tables was worn bare and the balls
were scuffed up. I should know because I earned free time
on the pool tables by brushing them, which allowed me
to play almost as much as I wanted to. Over the course of
that summer, I got pretty good at hustling and it became a
decent source of income. Truthfully, pool hustling became
a job for a while. Wake up, brush tables, make some money
playing nine ball, and then spend it. This was how I spent
my days as a fifteen-year-old.

Leaning on my earlier "career" of snagging my brother's comic books and selling them in Central Park, one
of my new favorite scams was to steal records from the
store down the street, head down Wilshire over the PCH
walkway and down to the beach by the Santa Monica Pier,
and then sell the stolen albums to tourists or other people

hanging out at the ocean. There were no cameras in the stores or cell phones to record anything. It was easy stealing and easy money. The second I got some cash I'd buy a little food and then a lot of drugs. And if I didn't score any cash, we'd sniff glue—whatever we could get our hands on at the time.

My mother saw what was going on and forced me to go to school, but I repeatedly got kicked out for causing disruptions, not wearing socks with my sandals, being high—basically disrespecting the entire idea of school. My anti-establishment, hippie credentials rebelled against anything that reeked of "the man." Within three months of starting high school I was kicked out permanently. At first, the school system and my mother agreed to send me to an "alternative school," which was a place they sent troubled kids, but that didn't work out. Then they sent me to a private school in West Los Angeles that had a more "open" education philosophy. That school wasn't for me either because it didn't matter how "open" the education was, learning anything is impossible if you're on less than an hour's sleep and you're high on a number of drugs.

Now that I'm a parent, I realize what this must have done to my mother, even as hands-off as she was. She tried her best to push me through an education, but no matter what she did, I pushed back. She even went so far as to have my biological father (who I had nothing to do with) talk to me to see if he could get me to straighten out. He had very little influence on my life up to that point, but he said something that stuck and actually had a profound effect on my immediate future at the time.

He said, "There are certain kids who are meant for college and certain kids who aren't. Maybe you aren't meant for school. Maybe you should look into a trade or something."

I was about fifteen when he said that, and I took it to mean that I wasn't smart enough to go to college. That negative idea followed me for a long time. To this day, I feel a real loss that I gave up on my education so young, but that's exactly what I did.

Sometime after that talk, and the tenth or so time I got kicked out of school, and the fifteenth or so time I got arrested, a switch flipped and I went completely off the rails. My drug use went up remarkably (even though I didn't know that was possible) and I buzzed out the entire world. At one point, one of my crew at the pool hall got a job on the loading dock at St. John's hospital and he was able to steal morphine vials. Those became a source of income (to sell) and recreation (shoot up). We set up operations at one of the disgusting tables in the pool hall and ran our little "drug store" as best we could without a sober brain among us.

These were dark, hazy times, and all the memories I have are painful or drugged out.

On one particularly horrific day, I discovered that I got hepatitis from a bad syringe. It was disastrous. I remember being slumped over outside the pool hall, vomiting all over myself until I passed out.

I was still just fifteen years old.

There was nothing romantic or redeeming about those days. It was a hell that I continued to inflict upon myself, and for a time I just…drifted. I'd take whatever job or small chore that came my way for money. I cleaned boats. In one of my all-time low moves, I took a short gig for a couple bucks a day as one of those guys who leaves brochures on people's doorknobs. I was assigned a neighborhood or a street and I'd go house-to-house leaving my little leaflet at the front door. Unfortunately, I realized in my drug-addled mind that if I knocked on each door I would know who was home and who wasn't. Then, once I got to a few houses in a row where I knew there was nobody around, I sometimes broke into the house to grab whatever I could find that I might be able to sell for drugs.

Whenever I think about the fact that I did this, and even as I type this, a sense of shame comes over me. Throughout all of my drug-induced stupor and the periods of my life when I was seemingly staring into an abyss of hopelessness, I always felt deep down that I was a good person and the only one being hurt by my actions was me.

But when I think about those break-ins, I realize I was only fooling myself. It wasn't true. I wasn't a good person then. I was entering a house where I wasn't welcome and taking stuff that didn't belong to me to sell for a few bucks to get drugs. It was a horrible way to live and behave and it only fed my erratic behavior.

The one highlight I had in my life at that point (besides drugs) was that whenever I found myself in real trouble with the law, the state would rent out juvenile delinquents like me to the forestry department and we'd become fill-in forest firefighters in the San Bernardino Mountains as a form of correction and punishment.

It was a thrilling and scary and wild experience. We'd show up with a canteen and a bandana, and a work shirt, pants, and boots, and they'd fly us in helicopters toward fires that had been burning like crazy for months. I can close my eyes and still smell that heavy, deep smoke that signaled we were getting near the giant plume and the burn.

The chopper dropped us at the top of the firebreak and we'd work our way down the mountain, raking and clearing brush. We'd sweat out half our bodyweight, and our feet would get so hot that it felt like the rubber at the bottom of our boots was going to melt right into the ground. The only thing that kept me going was that, when we finally got to the bottom (after dropping probably five pounds from the work and another two from pouring sweat), they served us a giant steak that would take up two plates. They gave us a huge baked potato and corn, and the whole time I worked I thought of that meal. It was a feast for a king—and for a kid who was scrounging together money on the street and ate whatever fast food or scraps that could be found. I felt like I was in heaven.

I'd usually see the same guys when I was sent to work with the forestry department, and I remember for the first time in my life having a real sense of camaraderie. We worked together to accomplish something and we did it. I was a part of a team and it felt really good, which was a massive change from everything else happening in my life. Unfortunately, my brief stints as a brush clearer were the only bright spots I had in an otherwise dim and disastrous existence.

Months would pass and I wouldn't spend a single night in my mother's house. I'd crash at a friend's place, or at some girl's house, or in the back of a shitty bar or wherever I passed out. For a brief period of time I was "adopted" by some girls I knew who worked at a massage parlor across from the old Tower Records on Sunset Boulevard. They either took pity on me or I supplied them with drugs, I don't remember, but for a few months they gave me a small room to live in right inside the parlor.

Drifting…

Drifting…

Drifting…

Occasionally, if I wanted to get out of town, I'd hitch-hike up the coast to stay with my brother Bob, who had been accepted to Berkeley on an academic scholarship. He wanted to become a lawyer and he was editor of the law review. Bob was always an intellectual and he had his life in exponentially better shape than I did. Still, he got into "the scene" in his own way.

"The scene" at that time was the atmosphere around Berkeley and San Francisco. In the '60s and early '70s, that was where all of the action was. The hippie stuff. The riots. The best drugs. The best scams.

On one of my trips to visit my brother, I came across a guy who was signing up people for Shell credit cards. I signed up for one and then went all over town looking for a hotel that would accept the credit card. Then I discovered that on the back of the card it said, "this card accepted at the Disneyland hotel." And believe it or not, I lived at Disneyland in a hotel for two or three months before they cut off the card. Back then, that would have been considered a long-term plan for me.

I don't recall the exact dates and times of my wanderings through Los Angeles and up to Berkeley or wherever else. Everything is clouded with the fog of being hopped up on something.

———

The lowest point for me during this entire time period (yes, even lower than being covered in my own vomit on the street with hepatitis) took place in Santa Monica on Colorado Boulevard. Back then, Colorado Boulevard was known as a real bad area, the kind of place that was littered with pawn shops and rundown liquor stores and a rampant homeless population. We hung out on that street a lot. It was like our second home base.

My best friend at the time was a guy named Greg. I'd only known him for a year and a half or so on the streets, but we hit it off. He was a little older than me, and he always seemed to be pushing the boundaries of the level of trouble we could get into. If we were willing to break the law a little bit, he was willing to break it a lot. If we stole a bike, he'd steal a car. If we stole one thing from a store, he'd steal ten.

One day he cooked up a scheme in which he'd throw

a rock through a pawn shop window and we'd all reach in, get what we could, and run away. It's what they call a smash and grab, I'd later learn. On this particular caper, Greg and I smashed the window and took what we could hold, and we started running away—all according to plan. But as we ran, we heard a guy shouting after us. It was the pawn shop owner and he had a gun—and he was firing at us!

As we sprinted down the street I heard a shout, and right next to me, Greg went down. He'd been shot a few times. I stopped for a moment, in shock. I thought briefly about helping or staying with him, but the pawn shop owner kept running and shooting, so I ran away.

Greg died on the street.

It easily could have been me.

Greg's death was a big blow to me and my pool hall crew.

One minute we were fencing watches and other crap that we hoped we could sell or trade for drugs, and the next minute Greg was dead.

You'd think this would have been a wake-up call for me.

It wasn't.

It didn't make me want to change my ways, but it did accelerate a fantasy I'd always had of one day having a normal, happy family. Despite all of my transgressions, at the very fiber of my soul, I dreamed of growing up and living in a nice house with a green lawn and the proverbial white picket fence. It may seem ludicrous, considering how I treated my body and my mind and my education, but it was a direct reaction to how I grew up.

I was raised largely in chaos and I longed for order.

Soon after Greg died, I met a girl and thought I had my chance to move forward on a path toward that "normal" life. At this point I'd been on the streets for nearly three years and I craved an anchor. A person. A place. Anything to keep me rooted and give me a reason to have structure.

When I met this girl, she was sixteen and I was seventeen. After about six months, when we were both seventeen years old, we decided to get married. Neither of us were off drugs, mind you, so there was very little clear thinking behind this decision. Marriage was just something I wanted to do in the hopes that as soon as I heard the words "I do," I would suddenly break free from drugs and become a responsible, hard-working citizen.

As you can imagine, that wasn't the case.

I attempted to enroll at Santa Monica Community College, but like all my other attempts at school, I failed. And so did the marriage.

We didn't even last a year, and as I think about it now,

there was a mountain of futility in what I was trying to do. I had no education. I couldn't hold a job and I couldn't stay remotely sober.

Why in the hell did I think I should be married?

After the divorce, my self-confidence plunged beneath rock bottom to the magma inside the earth's crust. I believed I had nothing to live for and I became laser-focused on one thing and one thing only: scoring more drugs.

While I'd argue that most people in my life considered me a lost cause around this time (and for many years they were right), the one person who never wrote me off was my brother Bob. At some point during my "best-friend-dying, drug-obsessed, getting-divorced" days, Bob had moved back to Los Angeles and taken a job with a big law firm. He was never one to reprimand me or talk down to me, and he let me live with him and offered guidance whenever I asked for it.

By this time I was nearing twenty years old and I was strung out and broke. On the latter issue, my lack of funds wasn't for a lack of trying to work. In fact, I had more jobs than I can even remember as I tried to break out of my homelessness and transient phase.

I held nearly every hourly job you could think of that didn't require a high school education: dish washer, bus boy, delivery boy, and everything in between. I finally found a job as a file clerk in the basement of a building, and it suited me just fine.

It was steady. I didn't have to talk to anyone. It gave me time to think. That job was the first step on my road to becoming a responsible citizen, and while I was still drugged out, I found some semblance of balance and regularity.

I moved out of my brother's place and got my own apartment.

Then, in 1974, my mother's third husband began talking to me about selling insurance with the company he worked for, American Income Life.

He'd been in sales and was making good money, and he told me he wanted to bring me in.

From my perspective, it sounded terrific, but there was also a lot of pressure. Nobody had ever gone out on a limb for me before. I didn't want to embarrass him and let him down, but something inside of me said that I had to take advantage of this because it sounded like something I'd never come across before: a bona fide good opportunity.

PART II

THE RISE
AND FALL

CHAPTER 4

Los Angeles, 1975

A heavy sweat engulfed my scalp and poured down my quickly dampening hair. My skin seemed to change color, getting paler by the moment and taking on a sickly quality. I wasn't convulsing, but I certainly wasn't sitting still either. When I tried to speak, the words would come out mangled or I'd swallow air as I forced out the letters. With my body and mind in torment, my best course of action was to sit there and shut up.

If you were a bystander watching me in this condition, you might have thought I was having an epileptic seizure.

I wasn't.

I was simply trying to overcome my paralyzing fear of selling insurance and closing clients. I was so damned nervous. No matter what I did, a horrific spell of anxiety washed over me when I first began meeting with customers. It was paralyzing, and the more I tried to control it the worse it got.

What the hell was wrong with me?

At first, I was nervous because I was trying to convince a stranger to do business with me and I was afraid of rejection. Then once the sweat started pouring, I got nervous that they'd think I had some kind of medical condition, which would make me even more nervous, because if they thought I was sick they wouldn't buy from me and that would make me sweat some more...and on and on the vicious cycle of stress and sweat would go until the sit-down was over and I'd perspired through my shirt.

I'd leave the client's house looking like the entire meeting took place in a sauna. It was a brutal experience, but that was how I got my start. I understand it may be hard to believe, especially with how things ended up in my career, but when I write the following you can trust that it is 100% true:

Not one single thing about selling insurance came natural to me.

Not the rapport, not the presentation, not the fielding of questions, not the close. Nothing. When I started out, the entire prospect of sitting down in someone's house to sell them a product felt like hiking up Mount Everest without oxygen or even the help of a Sherpa.

My first insurance job (during my earlier period of job hopping) was with a company whose name I don't even remember. It was a horrible gig. The company sold products aimed at senior citizens but had no inside information or relationship with the prospects. There were absolutely no leads in the company to speak of. The entire operation was built on cold calling, and it was an old-school, talk-your-ass-off type of sell, and it was really hard. I didn't last long.

I trained for a week.

I went into the field for a week.

I quit.

At that point in my life there was a decent chance that I might have been done with the insurance business forever. After all, I had a difficult time keeping a job (drugs), I was terrified of selling (anxiety), and from my one week in the field I learned that I was terrible at it.

But (and in hindsight this is a giant, life-altering BUT), my second step- father Mike offered to bring me into American Income Life, where he'd been working for about nine months and was having a great deal of success. In that short period of time he'd worked his way up the ladder to become a Master General Agent. When you started out at American Income Life in the mid-1970s, you first became an Agent, then a Supervising Agent, then a General Agent, then a Master General Agent, and ultimately a State General Agent. So Mike made his way three-quarters of the way up the totem pole in under a year, and he thought he could help me do the same.

His reasoning was two-fold.

One, at American Income you worked off of third-party endorsement leads. At the time, a vast majority of those leads came directly from a relationship with the labor unions that the company had been nurturing for years. Instead of just calling up someone and asking if they wanted to meet to talk about insurance, with American Income you were talking to a union member who had already received a letter about additional benefits and was expecting a call from you. That's a strong introduction and these were strong, strong leads.

As a quick point of reference, when I was with that first insurance company, I'd make a hundred calls and come away with two meetings if I was lucky. Once I got rolling at American Income, I'd make ten calls and have six meetings lined up. It was a world of difference.

The second reason Mike felt I'd have success at American Income is because he was, in no uncertain terms, a hell of a closer, and he agreed to train me himself. In a way he became the first real mentor in my life, and he showed me the ropes of not only AIL but the insurance industry as a whole, which was like the wild west back then. Yes, it was "regulated," but there wasn't a ton of oversight, and you could do almost anything—at least for a short period of time—and get away with it.

The company wasn't made up of a bunch of college graduates, that's for sure. There were a lot of old-timers who had either been with AIL for a long time or who came over from other insurance companies. A lot of times back then, a guy would leave one company, take a job at a new company, and then replace the old policy of his clients with a policy from his new company. Of course, there were laws that stated a client had to sign forms acknowledging that they were actually cancelling a policy and not "transferring it" to a new company. These old guys would get around this by telling their clients, "I can't advise you to cancel this policy," with a little wink. Then he'd sign up the client with his new company and not worry about the paperwork, knowing full well they'd cancel it at some point.

There were a lot of things like that back then. There were plenty of agents on the up and up, but there were plenty who cut corners as well. They wouldn't clarify things or they'd play fast and loose with the difference between whole life insurance and retirement savings and cash value. People would get confused but still sign up, thinking they had a retirement plan when they only had life insurance.

If you didn't explain it clearly and breezed over the details, people thought they could cash out at some point AND keep the insurance.

Nope.

But we were small-time guys. The rest of the industry had million-dollar round table deals based on the face value of the life insurance they sold. Ours were little policies: $8,000 face amount policies and things like that. But that was our wheelhouse. Our philosophy was that if you're a minnow, you don't go where the whales eat. We wanted to market to the people the big insurance companies weren't interested in.

It's also important to note here that this was a brilliant marketing move by the company's founder, Bernard Rapoport. Mr. Rapoport was heavily involved in politics and had a great relationship with the labor movement. When he came up with the idea for the Office and Professional Employees International Union to set up our offices and then have us become union members, it was a stroke of genius. This gave us the ultimate "in" with our niche market. We were union brothers of the union members we were selling insurance to. It was a perfect fit and none of the other insurance companies did this. We were a 100% union company talking to union members.

When we went to unions and asked to talk to their

members, our selling point was that their members would rather buy from a union company than a scab company. Most insurance companies probably backed all kinds of anti-labor bills and donated money to anti-labor causes. Not us. We introduced ourselves as members of the Office and Professional Employees Union and said that we were just here to explain an insurance benefit available to you. It was a really sweet deal and I knew it, which added to the pressure I was putting myself under.

Between my jangled nerves, my drug problem, and the pressure of not wanting to let Mike down, it took me three or four months to get out of what I'd call "survivor mode." During this time I started listening to tapes of motivational speaker and author Zig Ziglar. The first book I remember was *See You at the Top*, and his words provided me with a sense of calm. The funny part is that he was always bringing up God in his talks, and back then I didn't believe in God. My faith is very important to me now, but at the beginning of my sales career, I leaned on Ziglar for his positive attitude and his focusing techniques. He became a major influence on me and one day I had the pleasure of thanking him personally. But we aren't there yet—not by a long shot.

In those early days, we were only in the office on

Monday nights and Thursday nights because the managers wanted to make sure that we were totally booked up when we left the office.

On a typical workday I'd begin at ten or eleven in the morning, usually after a late night of partying and drugs. My territory was South Central Los Angeles, and more often than not I'd be one or two appointments into my day and I'd already have to start making calls to fill the slots. Back then we'd get a lot of stand-ups, in which you'd show up to a house and nobody was there. Or you'd get a one-legger, which meant that only the husband or the wife was home. Having a sit-down with just one spouse was a complete waste of time, because you'd get through your whole presentation and then inevitably get, "let me discuss this with my husband/wife." It was too easy of an out, so we just never did it. Our rule was to reschedule those appointments rather than waste our time. Between the no-shows and the one-leggers you could quickly find yourself with several empty hours during the day, and the last thing you wanted to do was head back to the office empty handed.

Instead, I'd drive to one of the diners in the area, order a coffee (or five), take out a roll of quarters and a Thomas Guide and start making calls in the phone booth to fill out my day and week. If you're unfamiliar with a Thomas

Guide, it was a massive spiral book that had the entire city of Los Angeles spread out on a grid and then printed in cross sections. The thing was two inches thick and weighed four pounds, but this was a time before Google Maps and Waze, and if you wanted to get around LA, it was critical to have.

It would take about twenty phone calls to fill in any holes or cancellations. Of course, we couldn't set appointments too far in advance or people would forget and you'd show up to an empty house, which was a total waste of time. On Saturday you'd make your calls for Monday, and on Monday you'd make your calls for Tuesday and Wednesday, and that's how it went. It would take an hour or two to lock in a day depending on whether people were home to answer the phone or not. The goal with the calls was to have eight to ten appointments every day. I'd try to have my first meeting at 1 p.m. or sooner, and I might have my last one at 9 p.m.. Keep in mind that we were dealing exclusively with union members, so we had people who were coming off of night shifts or about to leave for a night shift, so a 9 p.m. sit-down could take place before someone started their workday.

As I mentioned, I was terrible at every part of the sale when I started out: intro, rapport, close—you name it, and I was a flop-sweating failure. The way you got acclimated at the time was by spending a week or so learning your presentation, then you'd go out for field training with someone to teach you the ropes. You'd observe them giving the presentation until you felt comfortable, and then you'd spend the next three or four days cross pitching, where you'd do one sit-down presentation and the supervising agent would do the next. You'd watch him as he made the pitch and he'd watch you, and after each sit-down you'd have a post-mortem about what went right and what went wrong. I was lucky to have Mike as my mentor because he was really, really good. He'd walk into a house, take over a room, establish rapport, and the sit-down would feel like part of a casual conversation. But once the close came he was a master. Since he was so clever about building a fast relationship with the customer, he'd assume every close.

Are we signing you and your wife up today, Mr. Johnson, or just you?

Would you like to sign on for a $3 a week plan or $4 a week plan today?

He knew when all the "closing moments" were in the conversation, he would wait for them to occur naturally, and he'd pounce. It was a thing of beauty, and I couldn't have had anybody stronger to teach me. In fact, Mike was a charter member of the President's Club, which was a special club the company created for the top producers. Later, when I became president, it was really cool to know that Mike helped start that exclusive group. Of course, when I was learning the ropes from him, the idea of becoming president of the company was the furthest thing from my mind. I wasn't looking to become president. I was looking to get one sale!

At first, it seemed like I'd never get the hang of things, but once I got my nerves under control and I had my presentation down pat, I slowly began to acclimate to the stress of being in someone's house and pitching them insurance. In month one on my own, I was mostly a wreck. Month two, I was partly a wreck. By month three, I had a breakthrough and my daily ratio finally shifted. I began to have more good days than bad, and I started closing one out of about every six appointments. This was by no means good, but it was about a sale a day, and in my fragile state it was important for me to put some wins on the board and expect to end my day with at least one positive outcome. This was something I took from Ziglar: Make being positive a habit and positive results will follow.

He was right.

As my reps in the field increased so did my confidence. I also increased my repertoire when it came to making a close. I learned when to say more and when to shut the hell up. In fact, shutting the hell up was one of the most important things I ever learned about that job. When you get to the moment of the close, whoever speaks first loses. I learned that once the offer was out there, if I jumped in or tried to sweeten the pot by breaking the silence, the close wouldn't happen. But if I established a strong connection with the people at the table and gave a powerful presentation, I just sat quietly and comfortably at the moment of the close, and the sales rolled in.

Over the course of another month or two my sales ratio jumped up from about one-out-of-six to one-out-of-three. At that number, and with roughly eight appointments a day, I was averaging two sales a day. Little by little, my confidence grew, and by my sixth or eighth month my closing average hit about 50%. It was around this time that something dawned on me.

Holy shit, I might actually be good at this!

And I have to be clear here. It wasn't as if I suddenly became this smooth-talking, lock-down closer. I was certainly above average, but there were plenty of guys who were better at it and more natural than me. The difference was that I worked my ass off. I truly believe that at that time, I might have been the hardest worker in the company. I certainly was in my office and probably for the whole state of California.

American Income's *Spotlight* magazine would be sent

to our office each month, and in it was a list of the company's top producers. I'll never forget the first time I saw my name on that list. It felt like I was finally somebody. I mean, I actually had my name in print for a good reason, not in connection with a petty theft or juvenile arrest. It was exhilarating!

I became obsessed with the names in *Spotlight*. Month after month, I'd stare at the names on top of the leaderboard for motivation, until one day I opened up the magazine and saw my name in the top thirty. I immediately tore out that page and put it on my wall. I now had my mission. One by one I was going to pass every person on that list. And that's what I did.

With every new issue that came, I'd black out a name or two above me and shoot for the number that I thought I needed to get to the top of the list. For the first time in my life, I was supremely motivated and willing to put in the necessary time and effort to reach number one. I didn't slack at all. I'd work eight or ten appointments a day, seven days a week. One thing that doesn't sit right with me looking back, however, is that in order to keep my numbers up, I began to dabble in the gray area a little to close sales.

Back then when you sold insurance, you could play fast and loose with some of the supposed rules on what you could say and couldn't say—the "gray area." For instance, we worked on commission so we couldn't tell a customer that we were on salary. Of course, when people find out they're indeed talking to someone on commission, they become suspicious that you're out for your own best interest (a sale) and not theirs (a good policy).

When I discovered that people liked to ask if I was on salary or commission, I decided to head that off early by representing that I was on salary. I wouldn't say it outright, but I'd allude to it enough that they'd stay away from the question. I'd rationalize it in my head by figuring out the average number of sales I got in a day, and I'd break it down by hour. Then I'd justify my answer (to myself) because whether I sold to these people or not, I was still going to make the same amount of money each week, *therefore I'm basically on salary, right?*

It's not like we were worried about the Department of Insurance at that time either. If the customer had a problem, they were likely to call their union. But it didn't matter for me. I got really good at steering the conversations to the places I wanted them, and I avoided these issues as much as possible. I don't remember ever feeling guilty about small misrepresentations like that. I felt that I was doing what I needed to do because the plan was so good for my customers that they needed to have it. It was like a series of white lies we told for their benefit. Still, I really thought (and still think to this day) that it was good insurance and that we were going to pay it when the time came. Over time, I came to value how important this feeling I had was—and how important it was in anyone who had success at AIL.

In sales, having a belief in your product, in your company, and in the leadership of the people above you is critical. You have to believe in them and what the company stands for. You have to believe in the mission statement. A rock-solid commitment to that belief system has to be there for success to follow. If a salesman doesn't believe in his product, he can't hide it. Rather, he can't hide it *forever*. Maybe in the beginning if he's making money, but ultimately, it'll show up one way or the other and the people he's selling will be able to tell he's not 100% on board with what he's saying. That's a bad vibe to give off. Also, the more you truly believe in the product, the more confident you will be with your presentation. People like confidence. In the end, they're buying you as much as a policy, and the two go hand-in-hand. By this point, I believed in what I was selling and for the first time in my life, I believed in myself.

As my sales numbers skyrocketed and my name moved line by line up the top sellers list in *Spotlight,* some guys around my office and the office down the hall asked to hear my presentation. During that period at AIL, there wasn't a standard presentation, so the guys who listened to what I was doing told me that it didn't feel like we were selling the same product. I wasn't too surprised by this, because even though a solid presentation matters, what matters even more is how you handle yourself in the house. They could have taken my presentation word for word and still failed, and I could have taken their presentation, put my spin on it, and sold like crazy. I understood why they asked though; everyone is looking for some kind of sales magic bullet, *that one thing* that maybe they could do differently to double or triple their sales ratio.

Let me tell you a secret: There's no magic bullet. There's only hard work, repetitions, and motivation. Some guys have it, some don't.

After about six months on my own and with my sales soaring, management bumped me up to the level of Supervising Agent, which meant I was now responsible for showing a new guy the ropes and having them with me all day. This was not good for me for a variety of reasons.

First and foremost, I was still a drug addict and I liked my time alone to get whatever fix I needed to keep going. Having someone in the car with me felt like having a chaperone at a junior high dance. It made me antsy, and I felt like I couldn't be myself.

The second reason I hated being a field trainer was that it made me accountable in the house. I couldn't maneuver in that gray area that I'd become so accustomed to while somebody was watching me. It was stifling. I also felt a renewed pressure to close. When I was on my own, I'd grown calm and comfortable, and the entire sit-down was second nature. Suddenly, with somebody watching my every move (even though they were supposed to be learning from me), I felt hot and cramped again. I overcame it eventually, but it was tough.

Becoming a Supervising Agent also represented another milestone: For the first time in my life, I was in charge of someone else on a job. As you can probably guess, I had no experience managing people. The only thing I knew to do was manage down the way people managed down to me. If my boss yelled at me (which they often did) I would yell at the person I was managing. I didn't learn until years later that you motivate positively with emotion and negatively with data, and although you can be passionate, you should rarely, if ever, have to raise your voice in a one-on-one situation.

But back then I yelled. A lot.

What can you do? It was all I knew.

If I'm being honest with myself as I look back on this time in my life, the early field training part of my career was headed for disaster. I was flaky because of the drugs. I was paranoid because I didn't want to get caught in any of my white lies, and I felt unneeded pressure because I was in charge of managing someone and I was a lousy manager. I should mention here as well that one of the reasons I disliked training so much was because of the extraordinarily high turnover we had with new agents. One day a guy would show up to work and the next day he wouldn't. We'd turn over an entire office in a matter of months. You might spend one week or one month training a guy and then he'd up and quit. This made the entire process of training someone very frustrating.

On the one hand, you didn't want to put too much time and energy into a guy if he was just going to blow you off the next morning and you'd never see him again. On the other hand, if you didn't make an attempt to train a guy, he'd never get better and he'd never make money, and then your turnover rate would be worse. It was a real balancing act and you almost had to train on autopilot so you didn't get too attached to a guy who might quit at any moment.

If you're unfamiliar with insurance sales, especially the kind of one-call closing we did (which I'll break down in the next chapter), you may be wondering why we lost such a high number of people during training or shortly thereafter. There are a few answers for this. The first is that, simply put, sales isn't for everyone. It can be uncomfortable and stress-inducing. Some guys have no problem with it while others try it and hate it. That's life. No big deal.

The second answer is that you aren't guaranteed a paycheck. If you sell a lot, you get paid a lot. If you sell very little, you get paid very little. This inconsistency of income can be tough for people to handle. Some people thrive on working for commission and view it as the sky being the limit. Others have the opposite mindset; they view it as far too risky. How can you spend your day working and potentially not make any money?

These are both valid concerns, and plenty of solid people came through our doors who just weren't cut out to be salesmen…or at least weren't cut out to be insurance salesmen. But even if someone had the charisma and the drive to learn the presentation, and even if they were completely comfortable in a room, there was one part of the job that some people could not overcome or adjust to: the schedule.

In no uncertain terms, we worked a really tough schedule.

You were gone most of the day. You worked most nights. You worked Saturday or Sunday or both. If you were married, the time commitment was a real killer. What wife wants a husband who is gone from ten o'clock in the morning until ten o'clock at night, six or seven days a week? And if you had kids, forget it. You weren't going to be home to help with homework or coach tee ball.

We had plenty of nice young guys come in, but after one or two weeks of the schedule they quit because their wives weren't happy with the hours they were keeping. I don't blame them. As I think back on those days and some other parts of my career that we'll get to, one of my biggest regrets is not putting more of an emphasis on my own family, and not insisting that my agents put more of an emphasis on theirs.

The one saving grace we had, however, and the main reason we were able to retain the percentage of guys we did (whether they were married or not and whether they had kids or not) was that if you hit it right and you had a knack for it, you could make really, really good money. Truth be told, that's what kept me going in those days. Despite all of the obstacles—the drugs, the training, the long hours, all of it—I could still close and I could still make money, and when guys who drove around with me saw that, they wanted in. They didn't care about the drawbacks, they cared about the draw: cash.

The key to retaining the guys who stayed was to organize them and make sure they kept making money. A salesman (and maybe his wife or girlfriend) will overlook a lot of long hours and inconveniences if he's making more money than he ever has. So when a guy stuck with me, I stayed on him like glue to make sure he was closing and setting enough appointments and not getting lackadaisical once he had a few successful weeks.

Despite my shortcomings as a leader and my resistance to training people, I managed to be successful and retain a few guys. This was important because it allowed me to slowly move up the company ladder and get a new commission contract. From that first group of I was able to build my own management hierarchy and then over time, I was able to train them to manage agents as well. Before you knew it, you had your own successful management tree. It was a good deal if you could keep expanding and, most importantly, train your guys to keep closing. One caveat that I'll get into later is that if you wanted to keep moving up, you likely had to move.

Another byproduct of having some success was that I got to rise within the company alongside a group of guys who were on the same trajectory as I was. In that Los Angeles office there were five or six other guys who were doing well and with whom I hung out a lot. We'd go out to bars together and get high together, and there was a real camaraderie there that I hadn't felt since my old pool hall days in Santa Monica. This feeling of brotherhood is something that stuck with me for my whole career. In fact, a few of the guys from those early days were friends of mine for a long time in the company.

CHAPTER 5

The Art of the Close

What you need to know up front is that back in the 1950s, '60s, and '70s, a vast majority of insurance salesmen met with customers two or three times to make a close. They were dealing with bigger premiums and a bigger commission, so they could take their time.

They'd show up to the customer's house, ease into a conversation, get to know the family a bit, drink some coffee, compliment the wife on the pastries she made, crack a few jokes with the kids, and explain that he was there to get a feel for what kind of insurance that family needed. Then maybe that insurance agent would come back a week later and present what he thought was best for this particular family, and if he was lucky or good (or both), he'd get the customer to sign the contract. Then a week or two after that, he'd go to the house a third time to deliver the final, printed policy.

We didn't do any of that.

We were in and out of a house in an hour, and we didn't have the luxury of going back. Our commissions were smaller and our policies were smaller, so for us it was a numbers game. We needed X number of calls to make Y number of sales and that was that. It was a completely different mindset.

Point in fact: When I began the process of field training, I groaned every time I was assigned to an old-timer who was in his 50s or so and had been selling insurance his way for decades. In these cases, experience was not a positive. It was actually a flat-out negative, because the way they'd been taught to sell insurance was not the way American Income sold insurance.

I'd start to train one of these guys, and he'd say, "Yeah, yeah, yeah, kid. I've been selling insurance since you were a baby. I'll show *you* how it's done."

He wouldn't learn the presentation or listen to what I was saying, then he'd go into the house, take twice as long as we'd like, leave without a sale, and say that everything went okay!

I don't think so, pal.

These guys would usually flame out pretty quickly because it wasn't possible to whitewash an entire career of selling one way and teach them to do it our way from scratch. There was too much ego involved. And even the guys who said they wanted to learn how we did it never really could. I was fooled too many times to count, believe me.

So when you add up the old-timers, the guys who weren't cut out to sell, the married guys whose wives hated the schedule, and the general turnover you get in any commission job, you have to churn through a lot of people to find the 10% or 12% of salesmen who could last a year.

The other thing going against us was that, even when we'd get a sharp guy from another insurance company, the odds were high that he was too technical in his approach. He was likely used to wearing a suit and wielding big words to impress his potential customers. That crap didn't work with union guys.

Our business back then was 90% union workers, and these were blue-collar people. Some had high school diplomas and some didn't. The KISS approach (Keep It Simple, Stupid) was extremely valuable—not because the workers we sat with weren't smart; they just didn't have time for bullshit.

And neither did our agents.

In order to do our presentations and close in under an hour, we had to become efficient with our time, economical with our words, and keep an internal clock as we moved step-by-step through the stages of a sit-down, which I'll outline here.

Appearance

Before you even step foot into a prospect's house, you have to think about how you'll look to them at first glance. What is the first impression you're going to make? Our goal with American Income was to show that we were union members just like them. They didn't wear sports jackets and ties to work, so we didn't wear one to their house. All of our agents wore a simple pair of slacks and a shirt. We blended in. We looked like one of their friends, not a guy asking them for money.

Charisma

One thing that someone can sense immediately is whether or not you're confident and comfortable when you enter a home. After all, you're now in their house. This is where they raise their kids and eat their meals and watch ball games and gather for holidays. They have the ultimate home court advantage. If you're nervous or seem tired, they'll know it, and it'll make them leery of you right off the bat.

When I wrote earlier that I was awful at every single part of the sales presentation, that was 100% accurate. The *only thing* I had going for me was that I was blessed with being naturally charismatic. Once I got over my fear of knowing the presentation and I could be myself, I had a real ability to create a rapport very quickly. But even if a salesperson wasn't naturally charismatic, there was a game plan they could follow to increase their chances of success.

The Open

The second I walked into someone's home, my eyes began to scan the place like I was the Terminator. I was searching for anything I could connect to on a personal level—trophies or awards on fireplace mantels, framed certificates on the wall, or certain books on a bookshelf. These were easy to spot and identify. I also made a point to zero in on pictures of kids or family hobbies.

All I needed was something to latch onto that would help spark a natural conversation. Even something as simple as a picture of the family on the beach was enough.

That's a beautiful sunset behind you, what beach is that? Were you there celebrating anything special? Your anniversary? Get any fishing or snorkeling in? Oh yeah? I love fishing. What'd you catch? What'd you use as bait?

61

And you're off and running like two old friends catching up.

Controlling the Room

While you're talking about a client's vacation photos or their Dale Earnhardt Racing Camp certificate, you're also manipulating the room and taking control very quickly. Rather than let a customer suggest a place to sit down, I'd tell them where I'd like to have our conversation. Then I'd ask for something to drink, regardless of whether I was thirsty or not. I wanted to get them into the habit of listening to me and getting me things—a glass of water now, a checkbook later.

As I talked, I spoke to both the husband and the wife, but I was usually directing my eyes and my gestures more to the wife, because she was the beneficiary and probably controlled the checkbook. There were all kinds of subconscious signals that people sent as we talked. I'd look for little glances between the husband and the wife as I spoke, and if it looked like the wife called the shots I'd play to that. There were dozens of things going on at once and you had to respond in just the right way. It was kind of like sitting at a poker table. Neither of us had any cards, but I was still trying to read their expressions the entire time.

If I got a guy who was a real hard-ass and didn't want to participate, I'd find a reason to move the conversation to a different room. Change the scenery. Get him to accept my suggestions. The key was to slowly get him to listen to me. I had to establish dominance in the conversation and show that I was leading the discussion, not the other way around. I taught this to all of my agents.

Setting Up the Close

A key to our presentation was asking the customer a series of questions that would all be answered in the affirmative. We took the same approach that lawyers did when cross-examining a witness: Never ask a question you don't already know the answer to. The questions we'd ask were those that the bulk of the people we talked to would answer the same way. They were designed to get the client to speak their "yes" answer over and over. We weren't after head nods or silent consent. We wanted to quickly condition customers to say the word "yes."

Jim, we know you love your wife and kids, don't you?

Yes.

And of course you're worried about your family's future if something were to happen to you, right?

Yes.

We'd ask these types of questions over and over with slight variations, so by the time we got to the actual moment of truth, we had established a pattern of agreement and assent. When the time came to wrap things up, we didn't even ask if the client was interested, rather, we'd assume the close.

The Close

The most critical part of the assumed close is to never, ever ask a question at the end of your presentation that could have a yes or no answer. The last thing in the world you'd want to say is something like, "It sounds like you're really interested in our insurance. Would you like to buy a policy?"

Nooooooooooooooooo.

That's a disaster.

Let's say we've spent the entire presentation discussing a plan that could either be just for the husband or potentially for the husband *and* the wife. Instead of the example above that could lead to a quick, hard "no," you'd say, "Do you want to start off with the whole family covered today, or just half?"

The answer doesn't leave room for a "no," and if you've done your job from the moment you walked into the house, you have a good chance of walking out with the proposed policy, or perhaps even a lesser policy that we offer. But you don't start offering those until after you get a "yes" or "no" on the big-ticket item you're offering.

And yet, even if you establish an excellent rapport and knock your presentation out of the park, you will still have plenty of people tell you "no." This leads us to the next stage of the sit-down.

The Rebuttal

There are a million ways that someone can say "no" to a sales pitch, but they boil down to five basic rejections:

1. They can't afford it.
2. They want to think it over.
3. Their cousin/friend/whoever sells insurance.
4. They want to check their other policies.
5. And the catch-all, "Now's not a good time."

We trained our salespeople how to rebut each of the above with responses that corresponded directly to the particular rejection.

If they couldn't afford it, we'd say, "The policy I showed you comes out to about $10 per week. Would a $6 per week policy make you more comfortable? Or perhaps an $8 per week offer?"

You always have to assume that you can overcome what they're objecting to. If they want to check their other policies, tell them to go grab them and that you'd be happy to review them together and come up with the perfect complementary policy. The goal was to provide so much information and so many offers that they ran out of reasons to say "'no" and you walked out of there with something. In effect, you'd wear them down.

If you were doing your job, at least half of the time you could overcome any objection and leave the house with a signed policy to get them started, even if it was a cancer policy that we offered for around $4 per month.

That may not seem like much, but if you could rack up one or two of those every day as a "save," you're looking at real money in premiums over the course of a month or year.

The Button-Up

Once we made a sale, we used a strategy called "the button-up." This was our way of heading off any future trouble once the customer got their policy. We'd take out a specimen policy and go over it page by page. Then we'd take out a claims form, the beneficiary form, a sheet with information about the company, and a summary sheet of everything we went over that day. We'd put it in a folder (not including the specimen policy) and hand it to them, making sure they didn't have any questions.

This way, when the customer got the policy in the mail, they'd have a reminder that they'd already gone over the policy with us. The last thing we wanted was for a customer to get the policy and then decide that they wanted to show it to their cousin who sells insurance. If that happened, more often than not it led to a quick cancellation. The button-up was meant to build confidence and redundancy so that it felt seamless. A customer would get the policy, put it in the folder we left with them, and remember that, "I've been over all this, I'm all set." Then they'd put it in a drawer somewhere and pay it until they needed it.

When to Walk

Lastly, there comes a time in many a sit-down when you've run through all the rebuttals and you've taken a shot at a close three or four or five different times, you've been at the house for over an hour…and it's just not happening.

Most likely you've got other appointments stacked up, and you can't let one long sit-down that doesn't result in a close cost you valuable time in the next house. When that happens, it's time to leave. Once you reach a certain point, the law of diminishing returns kicks in and your chances of leaving the house with anything decrease dramatically.

The key is to never, ever look irritated or upset.

You stand up from the kitchen table, shake their hand, thank them for their time, and leave a card.

Take your loss and move on.

The fun part is that once you got your closing ratio up near 50%, you knew that, statistically speaking, if you didn't close one house you were very likely to close the next house.

That'll put a skip in any agent's step.

CHAPTER 6

Salesman of the Year

One of the overriding philosophies I've always had in my life is to force myself to do something I'm afraid of as much as possible to overcome that fear.

As I wrote earlier, I was terrified of carrying out the sales process in people's houses. How did I overcome it? I forced myself to make as many calls as possible until it became second nature.

It was the same with field training. I hated every part of it. But you know what I did once I realized that becoming an excellent field trainer was going to be the key to my long-term success at American Income? I requested a transfer to a different office in Northern California, where the entire job was field training. In that office the supervising agent was your manager, and all you did was field train every single day. The only way I knew how to overcome an obstacle was to face it over and over and over again.

Eventually, the field training, just like the actual presentation, became as ordinary to me as breathing.

In addition to selling and field training, there was another aspect of becoming a manager that scared the hell out of me: public speaking.

I hated it.

If I was nervous when I began selling insurance in front of a husband and wife in their own home, you have no idea how miserable I felt about the prospect of giving a talk in front of a group of people. It almost made me sick.

In that first office I worked in, we had agency meetings in which we'd all have to stand up and tell everyone how things were going that week. You could talk about the most interesting sale you had or a unique close you made, or maybe a tactic you tried that worked—anything that might help a co-worker. Unfortunately, once I started doing really well as a salesman, I was asked to talk all the time, and it was horrible. I'd start sweating the night before just thinking about it. I'd wake up with a knot in my stomach and it wouldn't go away. The more I worried, the worse it got. But I continued to volunteer to speak, until one day I rolled out of bed, went to work, and gave my talk without even thinking about it. That's when I knew I had conquered my fear of public speaking.

Around the time I overcame this fear, the stars appeared

to be aligning for my long-term future at American Income. Through my hard work and trial by fire, I was approaching a mastery of the main skills needed to move up in the organization: sales, training, and speaking. With my newfound comfort in all three areas, I began thinking long term for the first time in my life.

State General Agent, here I come!

One thing I knew that would put me on the map would be to win Agent of the Year. Every month when *Spotlight* came out with the top thirty salesmen in the company, I continued my ritual of crossing off the names that I passed. Each issue there were fewer and fewer guys above me. One month I'd be in the top twenty; then the top fifteen; then the top ten.

An issue that I wasn't aware of originally but soon realized was important, was the ability to write business that stayed on the books. The word we used to track it was persistency. If you had a good persistency ratio, it meant you signed up someone for a policy and they paid up front for over a year and hopefully much longer. If you had bad persistency, it meant that you were writing crap business and that you were signing shaky policyholders who would likely stop paying after a few months.

We had a big problem with persistency back then, which meant salesmen weren't actually selling people on the long-term value of the policy; rather, they were selling the customer on signing the policy that day— occasionally even telling them they could "sign up today and cancel any time."

This was disastrous for the company because American Income was advancing 65% of the annual premium to the salesman as commission. In other words, when an agent quit the Master General Agent was responsible for the balance. And if that agent had really bad persistency, the MGA was eating so many bad balances he could never turn a profit. Then if the MGA quit, the SGA had to swallow the whole debt. If that debt got too big, then the SGA's value to American Income was negative and they'd have to cut ties. That's why it was critical for an SGA to constantly inspect their business. As time passed there would be a lot of inspections of policies, but back then there wasn't, which meant that there were guys gunning for Agent of the Year who were filling up their sales with complete and total garbage.

Yes, they might win the award, but eventually that bill would come due along with a hit to that guy's reputation and American Income's bottom line. Then the company-at-large wouldn't want to advance guys who wrote shitty business, because then they'd train their people to write shitty business, and that was a fast way to go out of business.

That's why I took pride in my presentation and focused on the long-term value of the policy to the customers. I'd tell them that this was a long-term investment in their family's future, and I'd stress that over and over again as I talked. I wanted good business that stayed on the books for a long time—because I wanted to be with AIL for a long time.

To be clear, there were two paths for top producers (of quality business). One path was to remain as an individual producer. If you went that route, you'd continue to write business and maybe your individual contract would go up from 50% to 65% over time, and your renewals (which would be continuous payments whenever the customer made their premium payments) would increase exponentially over time. You could make a really good living that way. You were responsible for your own income, and that's it. A lot of guys stayed on that path and didn't want the headache of management. They wanted free to time to fish or golf or do whatever. Good for those guys. They wanted to write $100,000 a year or so in premiums and be free.

I didn't care so much about being free.

I wanted to be on the big money path, and that path went like this: become an outstanding producer and then transfer that to becoming an outstanding manager and get your own territory and then your own state.

Step one for me was winning Agent of the Year. Once I put my mind to that, nobody worked harder. Despite my addiction issues, I'd take ten calls a day, seven days a week if I could. My area at that time was South Central Los Angeles and Watts, and I had it down, man. This was a largely African-American community, and for whatever reason I clicked with the neighborhood and the people, and I got in a zone.

Maybe it was the fact that I was driving around in a purple Cougar (true) with orange wheels (again, true) and that I had a huge afro (yep, also true), but my closing ratio soared in that area, and month after month I posted big sales numbers until finally it was announced that I'd done it.

I became the company's top producer.

I won the 1976 Agent of the Year award for American Income Life, and up to that point, it was the most gratifying thing I'd ever accomplished. I wish I could talk about how this was a turning point for me and that winning the award allowed me to see what I could accomplish, and that it inspired me to get off drugs and kick my addiction and poor decision-making in my personal life... but I can't.

If I did that, I'd be lying.

The reality, as is often the case with addicts, is that one step forward meant about five steps back.

Yes, I won Agent of the Year and it was something I

worked very hard for. And yes, I was invited to the annual sales convention in the Bahamas to meet all the other top salesmen and to accept my award in front of the whole company. And yes, I fucked it up.

I was a young guy and going to the Bahamas meant one thing: partying. Hard. I met two German girls while I was there, and they were my kind of girls back then. They drank, did drugs, and were willing to chase the night as long as we could. I eventually brought them on board our cruise ship as my guests.

The news spread that I had some German girls on board and the Coast Guard thought we were harboring stowaways, so they came searching for them. This was doubly bad because, as winner of the Agent of the Year contest, I got a fantastic room on the boat, but in a moment of generosity, I switched rooms with Executive Vice President Joyce Lillard. She was a real nice lady, and she'd been stuck with a room next to the boiler room. I figured I wasn't going to be in my cabin much anyway, so I told her we could swap rooms.

Nice, right?

Wrong.

When the Coast Guard boarded the ship looking for me and the German girls, where do you think they went first?

They went to the room I was *registered* in, not the room

I was actually *staying* in. This meant that Joyce had to deal with the harsh knock on the door in the middle of the night and the questions from the Coast Guard, all while I was off partying. When word finally reached me that the Coast Guard was looking for the girls, I decided to book three flights to Germany and get the hell out of town with them.

The three of us landed in Germany the next day.

I missed the convention.

I missed the presentation of the award that I'd dedicated the last twelve months of my life to.

I embarrassed myself.

To this day, I can't justify what I did.

The only way to explain my decision to bail is that I was an addict and I made dumb addict decisions. This one included not only skipping the annual convention, but also spending several weeks in Germany to avoid the fallout—the firing—that I knew was coming.

I haven't mentioned the founder of American Income Life Bernard Rapoport much, because I hadn't had much contact with him yet. Mr. Rapoport would eventually become a mentor, a friend, a cheerleader, and for a short time, a rival. Ultimately, we had a very long and meaningful relationship, but back in 1976, he was the founder and CEO of the company, and he was pissed off.

I'd gotten into trouble a few times prior to the incident at the convention, so I was already on his radar. But when I brought the Coast Guard to the boat and then scrapped the convention, he'd had enough of this guy named Roger from Los Angeles. Sure, I could sell, but I was clearly a huge pain in the ass and my personal life was out of control.

The minute I stepped foot in my office in California I was fired. I asked my stepfather Mike what to do, and he said to lay low and then call Mr. Rapoport, apologize, and ask for my job back. A few days later, I called Mr. Rapoport and told him how sorry I was for my behavior, and he accepted my apology. I don't remember the exact conversation we had, but I do remember that he kept saying things like, "You need to be more responsible, Roger. You need to get control of your life. You need more stability, Roger."

I told him that I agreed with him and that I'd be a new man from that point on. He took me at my word and hired me right back. I was relieved. I didn't change my ways very much, but I did one thing to at least present the façade that I was interested in becoming a more stable, responsible person: I got married for a second time to a really sweet girl.

The marriage was annulled two months later.

She thought she was marrying a guy who wanted to

get married, but she was really marrying a guy who wanted people to *think* he wanted to be married. This is another major regret in my life. It was such a terrible thing to do, and she deserved so much better.

Back then I was so desperate to give off the appearance of normalcy, and so desperate to hide my addictions that I thought if I convinced this person to marry me it would be a smokescreen to who I really was. It didn't work. Thank God it lasted only two months.

Many, many years later, she agreed to meet with me in New York City, after I'd overcome my addiction—and she laid into me good. I told her how shitty I felt about how things had turned out, but she had been waiting a long time to tell me off and she needed closure. I suppose the only thing I could do to effectively apologize was to let her vent her frustrations at me in person.

But in 1977, that failed marriage attempt was just another in a long line of desperate things that I did.

CHAPTER 7

Oklahoma, 1978

It was rare for a salesman to win Agent of the Year two years in a row, because most of the guys who won wanted to move into management and advance in the company. In order to move into management, you had to trade a lot of the time you spent writing business for time spent training new agents. Once you aren't producing 100% for yourself, it becomes difficult to compete with the agents who are, in terms of total sales. It'd be like trying to win the award with one or both proverbial arms tied behind your back.

After I won the award, I set my sights on moving up and spent the next year as a General Agent, field training new hires and learning the business in the hopes of becoming a Master General Agent (MGA), which was one step closer to my goal of becoming a State General Agent (SGA).

As always, moving up in a company isn't easy. Not only do you have to perform, but you have to battle the inner politics and egos of those who are above you. At that time, the biggest hurdle facing a motivated salesman in becoming an SGA or even an MGA was having to either move to a new state or hope that the guy holding that position in your state would leave. This was difficult to come by because if you're a hell of a salesman or a hell of trainer (or both), and you're working for an MGA or SGA and making him look great by helping him hit or surpass his monthly numbers, he really doesn't want to let you go.

At the same time, if you're looking to move up and you're having success, the only way to move up to a better contract might be to force your way into another region or state. It was a real delicate balancing act from both the SGA/MGA perspective and the perspective of the agent. Eventually, it became a tug of war. As you grew your management team, and more and more commissions and renewals kicked up to you, you became more powerful within that office. Over time, an MGA might find himself in a spot where the majority of the agents he is relying on were trained by you and not him. That's a very uncomfortable spot to be in. At that point, it might be better to let you walk...or risk losing the territory to you.

In my case, I had moved up from agent to Supervising Agent to General Agent very quickly, but I had plateaued as a General Agent in Los Angeles and was ready for the next step (Master General Agent). At the time there were no MGA opportunities in California, so my stepfather Mike, who'd been having his own issues with our SGA, convinced Mr. Rapoport to let us take over a new territory in Oklahoma together.

Well, *not exactly* together, which I'll get into momentarily. The gist of the move was that Mike would take over the territory as a State General Agent (the No. 1 guy) and I'd be his Master General Agent (the No. 2 guy). By that point, Mike was solid at bookkeeping, organizing, and setting up an office, and I excelled at training and hiring and a lot of the grunt work to keep an office rolling. On paper, it would appear that we complemented each other well.

But that was only on paper.

Something that is important to understand as I explain how the situation in Oklahoma played out is that at that time in American Income, the system between the SGAs and MGAs and the parent company was broken.

When an SGA took over a new territory, he would essentially have to "buy" that territory by paying for all expenses out of his own pocket. He would have to invest his own money and pay for everything. That meant he'd foot the bill for salaries, office space, utilities, furniture, phones, and everything else that was needed to operate the business.

This isn't the part that was broken, though. The broken part was that when an SGA took on an MGA, he forwarded a host of the expenses on to the MGA. This meant that when I "partnered" with my stepfather Mike in taking over Oklahoma, as the MGA I was responsible for paying for the leads, the office space I was using (we had several locations), a portion of the ads, and a whole lot more.

None of this came out of my pocket up front, as I said. I would charge all of it through the company, and then they'd take it off the back end. Unfortunately, there were very few, if any, MGAs whose back end was lucrative enough to handle all those upfront expenses. As a result, MGAs would stop getting renewals because those fees would go toward covering their past expenses and those accounts were dead. It was sunk money because if you were an MGA out training, you weren't writing your own business and it would take a long time for the turnover to catch up to having a profitable stable of agents. You'd go broke long before you saw any benefit of becoming an MGA.

It was an abusive system that completely buried middle management. It also made becoming an SGA a bad investment. For example, if you were able to tread water or hang on long enough as an MGA to become an SGA, you'd still be responsible for your debt as an MGA, but now you'd be loaning out the money you were getting from the company as an SGA to *your* MGA, so he could then take on the debt you just finished accruing.

Now you're in a spot where the commissions you were earning—plus the renewals—were going toward paying off that debt. This set up a scenario in which you could leave the company and then the next year get a $500,000 1099. It was a bad, bad system, and to make it even less appealing, the company was charging interest on the debt balance!

The whole thing was ludicrous. When I finally became vice president of the company years later, that system was one of the first things that then-CEO Mark McAndrew and I got rid of. There were too many disincentives to count. We simply couldn't have a system in place where talented people had no chance to succeed.

But back in '79, I was stuck in that system. And to make it worse, I was learning first-hand how awful it was from the one person in the business I trusted the most: my stepfather.

When we decided to take over the territory in Oklahoma, Mike and I were both going to play to our strengths. At that point, I had never set up an office or handled the administrative tasks or negotiated a lease. I hadn't bought leads or helped build our relationship with the unions or bought ads—or done pretty much anything other than sell insurance and field train. The plan was that he'd mentor me on how to do all those things and I'd head up sales and lead our field training efforts.

This was a good deal from Mike's perspective because we'd move to Oklahoma together and he'd have someone in the family he could trust helping him run the business. From my perspective, it seemed like a good deal because he'd show me the ropes and I got to move up to MGA. Notice how I used the word *"seemed."*

At the start of our Oklahoma adventure, things moved along mostly as we discussed, with a few culture shock moments thrown in. One of the most memorable happened on my first day in town, after I'd driven my purple-and-orange Cougar nearly 1,400 miles from Los Angeles to Oklahoma City. When I finally arrived, I was exhausted, and the first place I wanted to go was to a bar. I found a nice little dive in the city, parked my car, and went in for a few drinks.

When I walked outside a few hours later, I smelled smoke and my car was gone. Turned out that some local guys didn't like the look of the car, so they stole it, drove it a few blocks away, and burned it to the ground. That was some welcoming committee! I remember thinking to myself, *I'm going to have to do some transitioning. Oklahoma City sure as hell isn't LA.*

I loved muscle cars, but I replaced the Cougar with a very unassuming car that fit better in Oklahoma. I found myself a small apartment in Oklahoma City and another small one in Tulsa (I'd be traveling there and running that office), and we got to work. Mike did his thing fairly quickly and had us set up in an office and got the infrastructure squared away. That part was easier than I thought, and once it was done, it was done. You lease a place only once and buy furniture only once. Mike's heavy lifting was out of the way, and after that he settled into running the books for the office.

Meanwhile, I was deep in the trenches. I was placing ads in the classifieds, interviewing prospective agents, hiring them, training them, teaching them how to sell and how to train others—basically everything that would fall under "management." I was also paying for leads, meeting with union members, and overall acting as the face of the agency. The kicker was that I managed to do this for our office in Oklahoma City *and* our office in Tulsa. I was either in the field or on the road, and I was running myself ragged.

And it's not like I'd gotten cleaned up yet. I was drinking heavily. I was out all hours. I was regularly on cocaine and painkillers and all kinds of other things, to the point where I got good at looking and behaving normally while high out of my mind. How I accomplished all of this with my body not quitting on me, I'll never know. One thing I had going for me was that my work ethic was so strong that it wouldn't let my body succumb to the abuses I was inflicting on it. It's the only explanation I can think of. Regardless of how many drugs I did or how crappy I may have felt in the morning, I pulled myself together to get the job done. And the truth is, I was doing an excellent job.

Within a few months, I'd found us some new agents that were producing. As time passed, I'd recruited a second batch of agents that the first batch could start to train once they had their licenses. Soon we had several layers of new guys, supervising agents, and even a couple of general agents. I was on the road constantly, keeping track of our guys, training them, and coaching them up when they needed it.

I came up with an idea to tell the new guys that they were the dragon slayers. Whatever it was that they feared when it came to selling—older people, younger people, people who had too much money, people who looked like they couldn't afford the policy—I called those fears "dragons," and I taught my guys to slay their dragons. I looked at that as my responsibility, and it became my mantra. It was my job to help them overcome their fears, and in that way, I became their leader.

If I noticed that a guy was slumping or that his numbers went cold, I wouldn't let him make excuses as to why he wasn't selling. Instead, I would go on the road with him and show him how to get past it. That became my key to leadership. I wouldn't just give out advice and hope for the best. I'd stay with my guys and show them by example how to get past their difficulties. Anybody who trained under me quickly realized that I didn't allow excuses or prolonged periods of under achievement. That was the essential ingredient. They had to know that not only did I believe in them but that I'd put my money where my mouth was and show them the way.

I actually indoctrinated my guys with this attitude when they started training, before I even let them on the road. Naturally, I wouldn't let a person into the field until they had their presentation down pat. In order to prepare them for the real world of selling, I'd have them train in a scenario that I called "running the gauntlet."

Running the gauntlet was essentially a role-playing exercise in which agents took turns presenting to each other and handling every type of rejection under the sun. An agent would present and have to respond quickly to objections and be able to close and close and close again.

We'd throw everything at them so that the rebuttals felt like second nature *before* they ever went into the field.

Once an agent was able to successfully navigate the gauntlet, they'd be cleared to go into the field and start writing business. We had a proven system that worked, and for the most part, we didn't want any freelancers. Other SGAs had different systems or different presentations at that time, but the method that I learned in Los Angeles and honed in Oklahoma was the one I took with me for the rest of my career. I knew that whoever was being trained by me or by one of my guys was following this exact blueprint. This made it easy to help people because I could jump in at any time and know exactly what they should be doing or what they weren't doing. The standardization made it efficient, and once guys made it into the field, our retention rates went up because the training had already weeded out many of the guys who weren't going to make it anyway.

While I was installing this system and busting my ass training every single one of our agents in two offices, Mike was sitting pretty back in Oklahoma City. He no longer went into the field. He rarely trained anyone. He was just hanging back, handling all the paperwork, and letting me do all of the heavy lifting.

And it really pissed me off.

This "partnership" that I'd opted into was beginning to feel more and more like a one-sided deal. One half of the partnership sat back and didn't travel or manage anyone, while the other drove all over the damned state, worked eighty hours a week, and took home a lot less money. I understand that Mike was the one who put up the money to get us started and funded the operation in the beginning, so it's not as though I wasn't grateful. If we were sharing revenue evenly with a 50/50 split, I think I could have lived with it, at least for a while. Instead, not only were we not on equal footing financially, but I was still an MGA and he was an SGA, and objectively speaking, I was doing 80% to 90% of the work.

I realize now there are about a dozen ways I could have handled the situation better than I actually did. First and foremost, I could have sat down with Mike and explained how I felt. We could have had a man-to-man conversation about my workload and how I perceived the supposed partnership and what my personal goals were. Then we could have hammered out a new agreement or discussed a plan to make things more equitable and build in incentives for me over time.

All of the above are reasonable options and what I'd expect a mature, professional businessman to do.

I did none of those things.

Instead, I let the resentment and frustration build inside of me day after day for months on end. And rather than talk to Mike, I began to plot my way around him. While I was on the road all over Oklahoma, I began to take an interest in the state directly to the east, Arkansas. From an American Income perspective, Arkansas was an underperforming territory and similar in demographics to Oklahoma. This got me thinking.

I bet I can turn around Arkansas like I did Oklahoma.

Slowly, a plan formed in my head that didn't involve Mike at all. I decided to approach Mr. Rapoport directly and ask him if I could take over Arkansas solo as the SGA. In my mind, this killed two birds with one stone. First, I'd finally reach my goal of becoming an SGA, and second, I'd finally be out on my own, away from Mike and earning the money I deserved.

I had a good feeling going into my conversation with Mr. Rapoport, but I'd be lying if I said I wasn't a little surprised when he said "yes." I was thrilled. This was what I'd been working toward.

Finally.

My own state.

There was only one problem.

I had to let Mike know.

When I did, he was livid. Actually, he was beyond

livid. He was completely and totally enraged. From his perspective, he took a chance on us, put up his own money, opened up a new state, and things were looking pretty good. He felt that I was not only quitting on him but that I was quitting on the family, since we'd moved together. In his mind, this was a chance to work with family, to have the business in the hands of people you believed in, and to build something together.

All these years later, I see that now and I totally understand it. In those days, none of that really mattered to me because I thought I was being taken advantage of in a big way. In my mind, of course Mike was pissed off that I was leaving because he was making all the money and doing none of the work!

The fallout was disastrous. It caused a massive rift in our family. For a long time, my mom, Mike, and my sister (for a while) refused to talk to me. They saw my move to Arkansas as a betrayal. From their point of view, I suppose they were right. But I also believe that the level of anger Mike had proved my point. One of the reasons he was so upset was because he didn't have anyone to handle the majority of what I'd been doing. I'm not bragging here, but there weren't many guys in the company who could do what I was doing, both from a results and workload perspective. I knew that and he knew that. At the end of the day, the split lasted several years and took an enormous toll on my family. It's certainly something I wish I had handled differently.

CHAPTER 8

Arkansas, 1980

Little Rock is a really pretty area that sits almost dead center in the state of Arkansas. The Arkansas River runs right through it and natural beauty surrounds the city, from the Natural Steps to Lake Maumelle to the woodlands out near Alpine.

Prior to taking over the territory for American Income, I hadn't spent any real time in the state, but I quickly found myself enjoying it. When I arrived, I rented a small apartment downtown right near an Applebee's, which was perfect for me because it gave me a place to hang out and drink at the end of the day. Back then I was drinking a lot, mostly because I was an addict, but partly because I was working so hard that I needed some way to wind down after twenty-hour workdays.

In the beginning it was a real grind because the territory was in such bad shape. After my conversation with

Mr. Rapoport about taking over the territory, there was still the matter of dealing with the guy who was currently in charge. In the old days, Mr. Rapoport would promise a territory to twenty guys in the hopes that maybe one of them worked hard enough to actually get it. That was a very old-school way of thinking, because plenty of times he found himself with several people circling back to him about taking over a territory they were promised—and they were all promised the same territory!

I understand what Mr. Rapoport was thinking: Because so many guys don't pan out, you might as well dangle the carrot in front of everyone, and then whoever earns it first gets it. But I disagree with this line of thinking for several reasons. The first reason is that word gets out quickly among MGAs and aspirational SGAs that even though you were promised a territory it doesn't mean you'll actually get it. This is a morale killer and forces guys to take a wait-and-see approach about what they have to do to advance. It also leads to the second reason I didn't like it: It devalues your word.

One thing I learned once I became CEO was that you have to try to keep your word at all costs. If you say that you're going to do something, you 100% have to do it. If you're all talk and no follow through—or worse, all talk and no action at all—you will lose your team because they can't trust what you're saying. Without trust, you can't get anywhere. Of course, there's always the caveat that as a company leader you have the right to change your mind if you learn new data or a new situation comes to light. But for the most part, if you promise a guy a territory that means you've created a set of milestones for him to meet, and when he does, the territory is his.

In my case with Arkansas, Mr. Rapoport gave me the territory before he told the existing SGA that I was taking over. Occasionally, if an SGA finds out he's being replaced, he may talk leadership into giving him ninety days to turn things around, but that's rare. Typically, once the decision is made, the current SGA is out no matter what. That's what happened in Arkansas. From what I remember, the transition was pretty quick, as the guy had been underper-forming for a long time. Still, no matter how quick the change is, there's always plenty of time for the agents loyal to the old boss to leave, and for the agents who weren't all-in with the company to leave. This means that there are barely any agents left when you take over, and the ones who are left are rarely the ones you want to keep. They're often dysfunctional and, at-best, mediocre producers. Essentially, when you took over a state back then you were likely starting from scratch.

In Arkansas, I was starting from less than scratch.

When I walked into that office for the first time, there were only two things waiting for me: bad attitudes and misfit agents. Both had to go. If this was going to be my first shot at running an office exactly the way I wanted to, then I had no time for stragglers. I don't recall a single agent sticking it out more than a week, which meant that I had to execute my own game plan from the ground up.

First things first: I needed agents.

In order to build up my workforce, I put ads in all the local papers and classifieds and recruited anyone I could get my hands on. I'd ask any young, energetic person I met in the course of my day if they were interested in working with me. I may be exaggerating a little bit here, but that was my mindset: find talent.

As I explained earlier, the churn with new agents was really high, so I had to get as many promising people through the door and into training as fast as possible to get to a sustainable number that would stay with me for the long haul.

At the same time that I was recruiting, I had to go all around town and introduce myself to the various heads of the labor movement. The unions, as I've said, were the lifeblood of our business at that time. If a territory wasn't performing, there were typically several reasons why: poor leadership, improperly trained agents, a sloppy office, and the icing on the cake was almost always a terrible relationship with the local labor leaders (if they had one at all). In Arkansas, the relationship between AIL and the labor force in the area was somewhere between nonexistent and awful.

The fastest way to turn that around was to introduce myself and explain that not only was I different from my predecessor, but that my entire operating philosophy was different. I told every union boss I met that I wasn't there to just offer insurance. I was there to be a partner and support the labor movement in any way that I could. I was basically saying, "I understand you don't know me, but let me show you over time how serious I am."

When it comes to working with the unions, trust is everything. Hell, it's the only thing. It's what our entire relationship was built on. In order to achieve that trust, you had to have what my friend Bill Becker, who was the president of the Arkansas AFL-CIO, referred to as a "bad penny philosophy." This meant that, as a group, AIL was like a bad penny: We'd show up any place the union needed us until there was finally an expectation that we'd be there. It was kind of a left-handed compliment, as they realized that since they couldn't get rid of us, they might as well work with us.

If there was a picket line somewhere in the state, we'd be there. If there was a labor issue somewhere, we were speaking up. I hired a public relations person whose sole job was to sell the American Income Life story to the unions, so they'd send out a letter on our behalf. That's all the PR person did.

At that time we had a largely female public relations team. I realize that this is a chauvinistic mindset now, but at the time, the best PR person was a smart, strong, attractive, charismatic woman who enjoyed socializing at functions. This approach was effective when it came to dealing with union leaders back then, as they were almost 100% men. Having attractive women represent us, talk to labor leaders, and open doors to secure our relationships was a smart business decision. As it turned out, many of the women became strong union activists in their own right. They'd give their presentations to the unions, and if things went well, they'd give you access to their member-ship list—which was the single most important part of the entire process.

Why?

Because when you're hiring a new agent and you're promising them a bright future with American Income, what you're really promising is that you're going to deliver high-quality leads for them to work. And those leads came directly from the unions. If you worked with the unions well and they provided you with a warm enough introduction, one of the hardest parts of the presentation was essentially done for you. You were already entering a house with good will rather than as a stranger.

At this point you're hoping to get a flywheel started. This means that if you're building a great relationship with the unions and they decide to start letting you meet with their members, the following happens: The AIL agents who meet with the union members are professional and personable and do a great job, then that union speaks highly of you to another union and you get appointments with them, and so on. Once that starts, things can improve quickly, which is what happened with me in Arkansas.

For example, I'd meet a union head. I'd do what I promised and support them and show up for them all over town. They'd let my agents get in front of their members, and the members reported back that they liked the agents and the insurance. It was a beautiful thing.

A byproduct of working so closely with the unions is that, because the labor movement was so connected politically, you'd eventually get tied in with big-name politicians. In the early 1980s in Arkansas, that meant one man: a governor by the name of William Jefferson Clinton. Within three months of arriving in Arkansas, I was at the Governor's Mansion meeting with Gov. Clinton. Mr. Rapoport was very politically involved and had a great relationship with the governor, which he was really proud of.

Years later when President Clinton was in the White House, an article was published that revealed the heavy donors to his campaign that had been rewarded with a night in the Lincoln bedroom. Bernard Rapoport's name was in the article. It was a negative piece about donors, but Mr. Rapoport didn't care. He was just so proud of his relationship with the president.

I didn't get to stay in the Lincoln bedroom, but I did meet with President Clinton many times. But more importantly, I successfully turned around Arkansas.

***

As I increased my foothold in the area, I once again attempted a semblance of stability and married my third wife Sandra, who I met in Arkansas (but happened to be from Oklahoma). After living in the little apartment by Applebee's for a while, we bought a nice house on a plot of land in the country. It had a ton of acreage with its own pond that was fully stocked with catfish. It was a really peaceful place.

Every morning I'd wake up and walk on the dock along the pond. I'd feed kibble to the giant catfish that would surface and eat the food. To me, they were like pets. I even came up with names for a few of them. I liked having the pond, and it was useful for my job as well. Most of the labor leaders in that part of the country were big-time fishermen and hunters, and they'd come to the house and catch giant catfish. There was a tree just next to the lake that the previous owner had hung a massive hook from, and these labor leaders would hang a fish on there and gut it right after they caught it. It was great for them, and I was trying to fit in with these guys, but I'm such an animal lover that it felt like they were eating my pets right in front of me!

We'd go dove hunting near the property as well, and I had to fake my enjoyment because, to me, that's a really gory hobby. But aside from the hunting/fishing aspect, Arkansas was a gorgeous, rustic area. And I loved the house. It was a modern ranch with long hallways and light pouring in all over the place. We bought a lot of artwork and put it up, and really made it our home. I have a lot of fond memories of living there.

During our two years in that house, I continued to grow the business in Arkansas. I worked every union. I worked every lead. I pushed and pushed my team, and it all paid off. In my second year I won SGA of the Year for a Small Territory, and I was the first guy to write a million dollars of premiums in an area that size. It was a great success story and really helped me build my reputation with the company. Mr. Rapoport was proud of my success, and I was feeling really good about myself, which in my mind meant that it was time to plot my next move.

The place I wanted to go next was Dallas.

I figured I'd conquered the states of Oklahoma and Arkansas, and in that area geographically, the place that made the most sense as a step up was Dallas. Not only was it a similar market in terms of demographics to Oklahoma and Arkansas, but it was one of the top ten largest cities in the United States when combined with Fort Worth.

Sometime after winning the "Small Territory SGA of the Year," I approached Mr. Rapoport about the move. He was supportive, so I began to make arrangements. I rented an apartment in Euless right around the airport. I was still living in Arkansas and making the transition when I got the place. When I arrived in Dallas, I had to take three obstacles head on.

One, there was very little labor there, so I would have to saturate the market as best I could. Two, there were no referrals at all, so the business was strictly lead returns. But the most important thing I learned was that the guy running Dallas was good friends with Mr. Rapoport's son. I knew ahead of time that if I wanted Dallas I'd have to go in as a partner, but I'd gone back and forth with Mr. Rapoport about a few conditions I wanted in place—namely that if within ninety days I brought the territory up to quota, I'd have the territory to myself.

Mr. Rapoport agreed, but when the ninety days were up and I had surpassed the quota, he reneged on the deal. By this time I'd started to really look up to Mr. Rapoport as a mentor, so this crushed me. It gave me a bad taste in my mouth about the whole situation. Not only was Mr. Rapoport not honoring his word, but the guy who was my supposed "partner," who wasn't doing a good job anyway, just happened to be a scumbag. He was the kind of guy who had a picture of his wife and his mistress on his desk. Within a few months, the situation became untenable. I didn't like the guy I was forced to partner with, and I was doing all the work to improve the territory while this guy sat on his ass. And he was still getting half the payout?

Nope. That's not for me.

In this case, I didn't let the situation fester for too long like I'd done in Oklahoma with my stepfather. I told Mr. Rapoport very quickly that after those ninety days I wanted to get out of there. I was irate and felt that I'd been lied to, and Mr. Rapoport knew this. I had placed him on such a pedestal, and when he didn't keep his word to me, I was shattered. I really couldn't do my job with the passion I once had.

And remember, by this time, I'd won Agent of the Year

and SGA of the Year, so he knew I could produce. That meant I had leverage, and I could sense that Mr. Rapoport wanted to appease me (if he could) while not rocking the boat in Dallas. I just needed to find a place where I wanted to go.

I began looking at *Spotlight* very closely to see which guys were failing, and I weighed the pros and cons of the territories. It helped that there was a weekly report that was sent to all the SGAs, and it included the production from every territory in the company. When I examined the list, I was looking for patterns. Was this guy having a bad month? A bad quarter? A bad year? I put together my own chart to keep track of the possible places I could go, and after a few weeks I had my new spot: Maryland.

I told Mr. Rapoport that I wanted to take over Baltimore, and since he knew how hot I was over the Dallas situation, he gave it to me. The next day, I packed my stuff and headed to the mid-Atlantic.

CHAPTER 9

Baltimore, 1982

The first place I lived in Maryland was a non-descript house in a town called Severna Park, between Baltimore and Annapolis. The town itself was situated near the Severn and Magothy rivers, and it was a real change of pace from the outdoor beauty of Arkansas. I think if I had been in a different state of mind at that time, we may have moved to a more picturesque location or a more impressive house. But the truth was, despite my upward trajectory at AIL, my life was spiraling out of control.

In the years between living in Oklahoma and Maryland, I had begun using cocaine heavily. Like most addicts, I started out using it fairly infrequently. Then drinking and other drugs I was taking couldn't compete with the high of being on coke, so I craved a regular supply. What began as an every-weekend thing became an everyday thing, which then became a multiple-times-a-day thing. Using coke at that pace not only increases your addiction but also becomes extraordinarily expensive. I had started making decent money as an SGA, but the percentage of that money that went toward drugs is hard for me to comprehend when I look back on it. The level of irresponsibility on my part was staggering. Being strung out and high and burning through potential savings is no way to behave—especially for someone who wanted to have a family at some point.

But that wasn't even the worst part.

My wife Sandra and I were having real problems because we were both battling our own demons. Needless to say, as we got our start in Baltimore our marriage was hanging on by a thread…and then I added a new wrinkle. I was introduced to crack cocaine, which is cocaine on steroids—so pile that onto the list of demons I was battling.

Within a short period of time living in Baltimore, Sandra and I split up.

I moved out of our house and into one of the first condo/townhouses that were built on the harbor. It was probably ten minutes from the inner harbor in a really industrial area. There was a lot of manufacturing going on and they put these condos right over the marina. It was a really cool place. My condo was three stories, and the top two stories had a gorgeous view looking out over the water.

It definitely had a bachelor pad vibe. I didn't even bother furnishing all three floors or setting it up. I was eating out all the time and working all the time, so I didn't spend much time there.

After we split, Sandra went back to Oklahoma and got herself cleaned up. I was still far away from cleaning up. In fact, when we split up, it marked the beginning of a period in my life I refer to as the "dark period," and my introduction to crack was about to pull me farther and farther down.

Even as I write this all these years later, I can't even fathom how I functioned on a day-to-day basis back then. It seems impossible now. I was on so many drugs and my priorities were so out of whack, but I suppose I once again relied on my work ethic to see me through because, miraculously, I not only continued to function in society but I thrived in my professional life. The only explanation I can think of is that no matter how hard I was about to fall or how poorly I behaved, God was still looking out for me.

———

One of the lessons I learned in Oklahoma was that, when it came to establishing yourself as a territory's new SGA, it could be a smart move to put your office space inside a labor-owned building. In Oklahoma we'd heard that the American Federation of State and Municipal Employees had office space to rent, so we set up shop there to be around labor. Some SGAs did this, but most didn't, and I understood why.

When you were starting out, it was great because it could really help you fast track a relationship with the local labor leaders, and it was good to have your new guys around the unions. However, once you really start to build your organization, there's a variable effect because you now have so many agents in close proximity with labor leaders, and you never know what they might say or do in front of a union guy that could be detrimental to your relationship. My usual pattern was to start out by renting office space in a union building, and then once we grew to a certain point, I'd bring all my agents to a new office space and make the union space the public relations office.

My public relations office usually had four people in it, and their jobs were to contact unions, get endorsements, and be involved in the labor movement. On the endorsement front, the goal was to get the head of that particular union's signature on our letter to the union members. Most of the time the union leader could get that approved on his own, and once we'd established a relationship it was fairly easy to ask for the endorsement. Occasionally, a leader wanted to present the endorsement to the executive board themselves, and we did everything we could to prevent that from happening. Boards were slow and inefficient, and too often if we weren't there to answer questions on our own behalf, the entire endorsement was tabled. The flip side was that if we had to go to the board and could represent ourselves, we would get an endorsement from the whole board, which in some cases was stronger.

It was also the job of the public relations staff to know exactly what was going on in the unions and to keep us posted on major events that we needed to be a part of, such as rallies or meetings or a particular issue being discussed at city hall.

But like I said, proximity to labor is key in the beginning, so when I got to Baltimore I decided to move us right into the teamster building. Much like when I took over Arkansas, there was very little in the way of real talent among the agents I was in inheriting. I think at the end of the day maybe four or five people stayed on, but that was fine because I had my system, and when I found my new agents, I wanted to train them my way.

Once I had my office settled and placed ads in the paper to recruit, I started hiring guys, and I needed leads for them to set appointments. When I got to Baltimore, I did what was common practice back then and bought the old leads that the previous SGA had. The trouble was you had no idea what you were getting with these leads. It was a real crapshoot. The leads could have been sold as active but were really leads of people who had already turned down the presentation, or they could have been run a hundred times. You just didn't know, but you had to start somewhere.

Either way, I bought the leads, and as I was making inroads with the union, my guys went out and worked the old leads for whatever they were worth. During the first few months things went as planned. The agents I hired were hitting their numbers and progressing nicely, and I was meeting all the right union guys. I was also learning that back in the 1980s, Baltimore was extraordinarily corrupt. I mean there was corruption everywhere. The cops. The politicians. Everywhere you looked, someone was doing someone a favor, or screwing someone over, or paying someone to look the other way, or just putting the pressure on someone because they could. I found myself on the receiving end of both types of corruption very quickly.

On the "good" side, my relationship with the labor unions helped me get out of trouble a few times. When I moved to the city I decided to treat myself, and I bought a hot red Corvette to zip around town in. Like I said, I was drinking heavily and high on crack most nights, and I got pulled over all the time because that car stuck out like a sore thumb. I was probably also driving like a maniac and deserved to get stopped. All told, I think I got three 'Driving While Intoxicated' infractions, and all of them would just disappear. It was really something. I'd get the ticket and it was just wiped from my record. Looking back, I should not have been driving under the influence, and it's a miracle I didn't kill myself or anyone else. But in my screwed-up mind at the time, I was just happy to have the tickets off of my record.

I learned about the "bad" side of the corruption from that red Corvette as well. The day after I bought it, I got a call in my office from the salesman who sold it to me, and he asked if I could go outside and call him back from a pay phone. At first, I didn't know why I had to leave my office, but then it dawned on me: I was so tightly connected with labor that there was a good chance the FBI or someone was tapping my phones.

When I got outside and called the salesman, he explained that after I'd left with the car, the FBI came into his office and asked if I had bought it with cash or if I financed it. They asked all kinds of questions about me and my job, and they scared the hell out of the salesman. That was when I knew how deep the corruption ran.

I used to go to an Irish pub on a regular basis, and FBI agents would follow me in and sit nearby and stare at me.

I never knew if they were doing that to mess with me or if they were seriously following me. The truth was it didn't matter. The labor union was connected to the politicians, and the politicians were probably playing both sides of the law with the FBI and the mob and whoever else, and just by being hip-to-hip with labor, I was involved on some level.

Despite the surveillance and the drugs, I managed to turn the office around and meet the quotas I was supposed to meet, but because of the way AIL was set up back then, I was running out of money to fund the operation. Also, my old habit of letting problems fester had popped up again, and I couldn't get over how Mr. Rapoport had reneged on giving me Dallas. Yes, I got another territory in Baltimore, and yes, I should have been able to move on and be professional about it, but I simply couldn't.

I think part of the problem was that I looked up to Mr. Rapoport as a mentor, and when you put someone on a pedestal like that, they can never live up to it. In some cases, mentors show you ways that you should behave, and at the same time teach you ways not to behave. In that case, I learned how not to behave as a leader, and I put that in the back of my mind for when (if) I was ever in his position. The truth was that the last thing I needed at that time was to be holding a grudge.

There were a lot more pressing issues I should have been focused on.

In no particular order: My third marriage was over; I was on crack; I was high or drunk or both most of the time; I was out of cash; My mind was a mess; I was barely getting by on a daily basis, and it took every ounce of energy I had to pass myself off as a functioning businessman. Eventually, all of the above began to make me feel like the walls were closing in, and I realized I needed to get the hell out of Baltimore.

I called Mr. Rapoport, and the solution we came up with was to make me a Regional Director of the company. I was cash poor and needed some money to make the move, so I sold the furniture that I'd bought from the old SGA in Baltimore. Under AIL's old business model (that I eventually replaced), it could take three or four years for an SGA to get out of debt to the company. Remember, when an SGA took over a new territory, the company advanced all the money needed to operate.

When it came to paying your agents, you're collecting a one-month premium but you're advanced nine months of commission on each sale to pay out, so multiply that by the number of sales and agents you have, and the numbers can become pretty staggering pretty quickly. Everything you paid out as an SGA was advanced to you, so if you had negative persistency—which you would in a new market, at least for a little while—getting out of debt to the company could take even longer. On top of that, everything was a back-end charge. The salaries you were paying your PR people, the bonuses you were paying your agents—all of it went to the back end of your contract, and these accounts might not clear for five or six years. In the interim, you were making money on paper, but you were also sort of broke at the same time. It was a screwy set-up, and that's why I sold the office furniture when I was thinking about moving and needed to get some quick cash.

Once I had the proceeds from my sale, I began to make arrangements to leave Baltimore for my new job. One of the first steps was a trip down to Waco, Texas to go over my new responsibilities and discuss the transition. When I landed, I thought I'd be in meetings all day to discuss my goals as the Regional Director.

Instead, I got fired.

I knew something was wrong when I showed up and, instead of meeting with Mr. Rapoport, I met with the company hatchet man, a vice president by the name of Fred Hudson. If you were meeting with Fred, you knew you were toast. Fred told me that since American Income Life had financed my move to Baltimore, I didn't have the right to sell the furniture since it wasn't technically mine.

Because the furniture wasn't mine, the proceeds from the sale weren't mine either, which from their point of view made it look as if I'd sold company furniture for personal profit.

Even though I met the quotas I was supposed to meet, and I did everything I said I was going to do, and even though the new position I thought I was taking was still with American Income Life, they terminated me. They were the "bank," and I "stole" from the bank. I obviously didn't see it that way at the time because I wasn't leaving the company, and the mingling of my salary and commissions and loans and paybacks through AIL was beyond confusing, but at the end of the day, I have to take the blame. Selling the furniture was stupid, and I paid the price.

Looking back, the furniture issue wasn't why I was really fired. I was fired because reports had no doubt gotten back to AIL leadership that I was totally out of control. I brought drugs to the office. I allowed drug usage in the office. I did drugs with my leadership team. I absolutely deserved to be terminated.

Now, rather than starting a new job to help me get the bad taste of Dallas out of my mouth, I had no job and a firing to add to my distaste for AIL. It's safe to say that I was circling the drain at this point in my life. But I had one more lifeline before I'd completely crater.

CHAPTER 10

Rock Bottom in Los Angeles, 1985

Desperation is a funny thing. It can bring out the best in you, or it can bring out the worst. When I got back to Baltimore after losing my job, I can say for certain that my desperation was throwing gasoline on the fires of my inner demons. Sure, I'd been a junkie for a long time, but at least I was a successfully employed junkie. Being an unemployed junkie has an entirely different feel to it, and for the first time in a long time, I felt like I was in real trouble. During my decade or so with American Income, I'd made the insurance business part of my identity. In fact, it was one of the only parts of my identity that I was proud of because it was the only thing I was good at.

Now that was gone.

Taking stock of my life at that point, I had a few minor

things going for me. The first was that I'd met another woman, Dottie, who would soon become my fourth wife and was committed to staying with me wherever I went after Baltimore. The second was that I had reconciled with my stepfather, and he helped me with my exit from AIL. He also offered us a place to stay in Los Angeles if we needed it…and of course, we did. But the same problem remained as before: I had no money.

In one of my more questionable moves to raise cash, I decided to sell leads from policyholders to somebody who had been in the organization in Baltimore. I knew some people had done that in the past, and it clearly wasn't right. In fact, you sign a contract with American Income that says you would never do that. The minute AIL found out about it, they sued me. Then my brother had to get involved to countersue them, and fortunately the whole thing was dropped fairly quickly. Still, I had continued my destructive pattern of burying myself deeper and deeper with each move. I wasn't one step forward, two steps back; I was two steps forward, ten steps back.

While I was trying to figure out my next step, I remembered that six or seven of the big SGAs from American Income had left the company a year earlier to form another company. I reached out to them and they offered me the chance to open an office in Los Angeles. I jumped at it.

Truth be told, it was my only option. I may or may not have had a non-compete with AIL at the time, but it didn't matter to me because I had nothing to lose.

Dottie and I drove across the country from Baltimore to Los Angeles with everything I owned in my car. In a way it was reminiscent of when my first stepfather Andy had packed up the whole family in the station wagon and moved us from New York to California. Even though I was the adult this time, I was moving to the West Coast for a fresh start, just like he did, and I was in an eternal struggle with my own demons, much like he was. And to add to the parallel, I was fleeing a disastrous business failure in the hopes of restarting my career on the Pacific side of the country. I was even moving to Malibu.

––––––––

For the first three months in California, Dottie and I lived with my mom and Mike in a guest bedroom in their house on the Pacific Coast Highway. This was the first time I'd spent any real time in Malibu since I was a teenager, back when life was carefree and sober. Now, I was in debt and a drug addict, headed toward a fourth marriage, and looking to make a quick score with my new job.

When I went to meet with the guys at the new company, which they'd named Union Life Insurance Services, I decided to bring Mike in again as my partner. We opened up an office on 5th and Wilshire. I basically did the same thing I'd always done: I went out, contacted unions, started hiring agents, etc… It was similar to American Income. Once we started building, we were doing pretty well and the business was paying for itself. Mike and I were even able to take a weekly draw out of the business.

After several months, we were in a strong growing phase, but the rest of the company wasn't doing very well. I vividly remember being at their first convention in Spain and the president of the company saying to me half-jokingly, "I'm not so sure that next year we won't be having our convention in a phone booth."

As the job rolled on, Dottie and I moved into a cottage in Malibu that was like a small gatehouse. It was a decent place, but it was tiny, and even though I hoped to make more money and get us a larger place, I was increasingly realizing that that wasn't going to be possible, because being back on the West Coast had only made my addictions worse. I lived every day with one thing on my mind: to smoke crack and buy more crack. This was hard to do when I was bringing in money as an SGA, and it was damn near impossible to do when I was trying to make things work with this new agency. The bottom line was that I didn't have the money to score the drugs I was addicted to.

That's a scary, scary place to be, man, let me tell you.

I remember one night sitting on the floor of our cottage at about three in the morning. I was sweating and exhausted, and my fingertips were worn raw because I'd spent about four hours picking at this crappy rug in our place to see if I'd dropped even the tiniest shard of crack in the fabric. My face was inches from the carpet, and I pulled apart all the little threads. I was paranoid and frustrated and I hated myself. As I pawed through the carpet, I thought, *I can't keep going on like this. I'm going to walk into the ocean and drown.*

This thought rolled through my head all night.

Just walk into the ocean and don't stop. Put your misery behind you.

I was thirty-six years old, and for the first time in my life I had reached a point where I wasn't even sure what I was living for. I contemplated walking into the ocean all night long, and when the sun came up, I realized that since I hadn't done it, maybe I didn't want to die. Looking back, this was clearly an instance of God watching over me, because it was clear that I couldn't continue to live how I'd been living, so I spent all morning making phone calls to rehab facilities.

Nowadays you can go online and find a rehab facility in about two seconds, but back then it wasn't easy to find one that your insurance would take. After a few hours of calling around, I found a facility in Napa Valley, set up my arrival, and booked a plane to get there.

The next day when I got on the plane, I was trembling I was so nervous. I could barely hold it together, so I decided that if I was going to get sober I'd first go out with a bang. I drank every bottle of alcohol on that plane, and I was a staggering mess when the plane landed. After we were on the ground, we had to take a bus to the facility. I remember stumbling to the bus stop and the bus having already started to leave.

Even in my hazy state, I knew that if I missed that bus it was over for me. So I ran toward the bus in what probably looked like an out-of-shape, drunk gallop, and thankfully the driver saw me and stopped. That moment changed my life forever.

Over the next forty-five days, I treated rehab like I did every job I ever had at American Income—I worked my ass off. For so many years, my work ethic was probably the only thing that kept me alive, and at this point, perhaps it saved my life. I wanted more than anything in the world to rid myself of these demon addictions, and I tackled every step they gave me with everything I had.

My stay in the facility was extremely intense and extremely supportive, and I remember it fondly. By the time I was ready to leave, I had reversed how I did every single thing in my life. I was going to do away with all of my old habits by doing away with the old me. If I used to put on my socks left foot first, now I was going to put on my right sock first. If I brushed my teeth with my right hand, I was now going to use my left. It was an entire reprogramming of my life and all of my habits, and it was exactly what I needed.

Meanwhile, during my time in rehab, Mr. Rapoport reached out and told me to get in touch with him when I got out. He was giving me a second chance, and in my heart, after I had finally let go of all the anger I'd built up for him, I decided to give him a second chance as well. That meant that my second chapter with American Income was about to begin…and it was going to begin sober.

Being sober provided me with mental clarity for the first time in what felt like decades, but it also brought on some confusion. During rehab I'd bought in completely to the idea that I had to change the way I lived my entire life, but I also needed to set myself up for success outside of work. At that point I couldn't manage myself, let alone a group of people.

On the one hand, I had tremendous success at American

Income despite my addictions. On the other hand, was it smart for me to return to the lifestyle and the job where I was comfortable working as an addict?

The old advice to "avoid temptation at all costs" was at the front of my mind when I left the rehab facility. The last thing I wanted to do was put myself in a position to repeat the same mistakes. However, I had one overriding, lingering thought:

If I won Agent of the Year and SGA of the Year when I was drugged out and frazzled half the time, how far could I go in my career if I was thinking clearly?

That was my mindset when I finally had my phone call with Mr. Rapoport and he offered to fly me to Waco to talk about rejoining American Income. Of course, I took him up on his offer (because I was broke), and when I walked into his office he said, "Look, there are eight different states I could give you. Which one do you want?"

I had a feeling this question was coming, and as much as I wanted to dive back in at the top of the food chain, I knew deep down that it was a bad idea. I was only a few weeks out of rehab and I was still relearning how to live my life. I knew it was going to take some time to discover how to be this new, sober version of me.

"With all due respect, for right now, I just want to go out and personally produce," I told Mr. Rapoport. "I don't want to worry about managing anybody or recruiting or running an office. I just want to focus on myself and personally produce as an agent in Los Angeles."

He understood and gave me his blessing to pursue that position. Fortunately, I'd been on good terms with the SGA there, a good guy named David Cohen, so I got in touch with him and told him what I wanted to do, and he got on board.

Believe me, there were plenty of SGAs who wouldn't have wanted me hanging around their office or working for them. I had a reputation at that time—both good and bad—but one of the things I was known for was taking over a territory. David was secure in his position, and he agreed to give me whatever support I needed to be on my own and work my way back.

There also was one other major discussion that I had to have, and that was with my stepfather Mike. Once I realized that I couldn't lead anybody, it also dawned on me that I could no longer work with Mike. And so, I told him I was quitting our partnership.

I knew he'd be upset, but it would've been a huge disservice to myself, to the company, and to Mike if I had stayed on. I was also concerned about being able to keep my sobriety with that kind of pressure. Nevertheless, for the second time in a decade, I left him holding the bag on an insurance company. He had to deal with the lease and the furniture and the staff, and it was a complete mess for him. Rightfully so, he was livid with me. And just as before, this turn of events caused a fight in our family and we didn't talk for almost seven years. At the time, even though I knew the damage it might cause, I also knew that I was in no state of mind to be running an agency. I needed to be on my own.

In hindsight, the decision to fly solo after rehab was the right one. By then I could do the presentation in my sleep, and since I wasn't training anybody or worrying about persistency or how other people were closing, I was able to do the job and go home. That part of my life was refreshing. The part that wasn't so enjoyable was that people who associated with me during my drug addiction days were constantly trying to get in touch with me. Dealers were calling me all the time and offering me drugs. The guys I used to get high with called me a lot. It was like a constant pull from my old life trying to suck me back in.

I never caved, but after six months or so, I realized that I had to get out of that environment and start fresh. Around that time there was an SGA meeting for American Income, and even though I wasn't an SGA, Mr. Rapoport invited me anyway. Let me tell you, just about nobody was happy to see me there because rumors had been swirling that I was going to become an SGA again, and that meant I was going to replace someone in that room.

When I arrived, I was nervous as hell. In fact, I brought Zig Ziglar's book *See You at the Top* as a sort of support mechanism. I held on to that book the whole time I walked through the meeting. Even though I'd been Agent of the Year, and I'd been an SGA, I was feeling so alone because I'd never done anything big with the company while I was sober. I felt like a stranger, somehow.

People were judging me. People were whispering about me. And people were clearly not sure what to think. Overall, I sensed a lot of suspicion about my presence. I did have a few allies, though.

An SGA who had become a good friend of mine, Eric Giglione, was one of the only people to come up to me. He could see that I was uncomfortable, and he said, "Glad you're back."

That meant the world to me, and as I made my rounds I held on to Ziglar's book. At the end of the convention, I had a long meeting with Mr. Rapoport, and we decided, "Let's do this all over again, and let's do this right."

He told me to get licenses in Chicago, St. Louis, Boston, and a few other places, but I already knew that I wanted to go to Chicago. I felt that the city was exploding with potential. It had a massive population. The demographics were great. It was a major union town. And to make it more appealing, it wasn't being run very well from an American Income perspective, so there was plenty of upside and room to grow. Mr. Rapoport agreed, and by the end of the convention they gave me the territory. They were also going to give me $2,500 before my move to help me out and another $2,500 when I got there.

Well, you're not going to open up a giant territory like Illinois with just $2,500 seed money, so I took one last gamble, literally. When I got back to Los Angeles I took all $2,500 to Las Vegas to see if I could increase my Chicago start-up money. I got myself a tiny, two-bit motel room and then headed to Caesar's. Back then I was heavy into blackjack, and I got myself on a nice little hot streak. Over a few days I took that $2,500 and turned it into $12,000. I called Dottie and told her to pack our stuff in Los Angeles and meet me in Vegas so we could drive on to Chicago. I had the money I needed to start.

A quick, funny story about that drive: When we were about forty-five minutes out of Vegas, I counted my money and realized that I had only $10,900. At first I thought I had miscounted, but then I remembered that I left the last batch of money that I won (which I'd put away for rent money) in the drawer at that crappy motel. Now, the odds of a stack of cash not being taken out of a drawer by housekeeping or the next person in the room in Las Vegas were astronomically low, but it was a lot of money, so we drove back.

Guess what?

The money was still there!

It was a small thing, but I felt like I had a little luck on my side. Once we picked up the money, it was on to Chicago.

PART III

CLEAN
AT LAST

CHAPTER 11

The Chicago Comeback, 1986

We arrived in Illinois in the dead of winter and immediately secured a room at the illustrious Silver Stallion motel in Des Plaines, which was about forty minutes outside of Chicago. The frigid temperatures and frosty environment were a far cry from our little cottage in Malibu, believe me. We chose Des Plaines because the existing American Income office was there at the time, and we chose the motel because we needed a place to stay while we got situated, and I didn't need anything fancy. There was a lot happening at this time in my life, and I didn't want to rush into moving to the wrong place or signing a bad lease or doing anything I couldn't quickly pivot from or get out of.

Also, Dottie was pregnant, so I wanted to make sure we lived in the right spot when the time came for her to have our child. Overall, I was excited about the move and what it represented for me. I also thought that I was inheriting the best public relations guy in the company. His father was the president of Amalgamated Bank, which was the union's preferred bank in the city. There was a huge Service Employees International Union there, and the paperwork in the office showed that there were all these quality leads. It was a giant list of names and at first glance it appeared he was doing great. His name was always mentioned as a top PR guy, so I figured I'd walk in there with a boatload of leads.

Wrong.

Almost as soon as I got into the office, I found out that the names were just a list of members and they weren't qualified leads—just people who were receptive to us calling and getting an appointment. Even worse, the unions had boycotted American Income Life because of some awful sales practices that the company had used several years earlier. They wouldn't even take our calls.

Immediately, this became my number one priority. If I couldn't repair our relationships with the unions, I was dead in the water. The strategy I came up with was similar to what I'd done in Oklahoma, Arkansas, and Baltimore—I got right out in front and introduced myself to every union person I could find. I also hired four or five new PR people, including my then-wife Dottie, who was a key member of the team. She was involved and committed and did great work helping us get started.

Our plan was to basically reset our relationships with the unions by acknowledging the sins of the past American Income group, and simply ask for a chance to show them that we were different. One of the big decisions I made was to move the office into the Teamsters Hall so that we could connect better with the unions. As it turned out, it was the Teamsters president who ended up giving us a second chance.

Once he did that, I ran the same playbook I'd run in other cities to show the unions that we were on their side. We showed up at rallies. We showed up at demonstrations. We spoke out at events. If the union was showing up somewhere so was American Income. And because Chicago was a big union town, the payoff was enormous.

Once things got rolling, we moved out of the Silver Stallion motel and into a great condo on Lakeshore Drive overlooking Lake Michigan. That was a really beautiful place, and my daughter Emily ended up being born there.

Working in Chicago was unlike any experience I'd had to that point with American Income, because about 30% of the unions were still under some type of mob control. They always wanted money, and they were on the take—something I refused to do. In what I thought was a clever strategic move (but ended up being a clearly stupid move), I hired a guy named One-Eared Frankie to work for me. I figured hiring this guy would at least get me into a few unions, but it turned out that old One-Ear was on the Top Ten FBI list for racketeering and everybody knew who he was. When he'd knock on the door for a presentation, everyone would go running. Evidently, he was part of the old crew that had been in Chicago for generations. A lot of the unions in Chicago were passed down from father to son.

The son from the younger generation was often trying to run a clean operation, but since his father was known for being a mobster, it was difficult. Still, to me, it wasn't a matter of "if" the unions were going to work with us again, it was a matter of "when."

And once the "when" happened, we really took off. I should mention here that the previous SGA, Phil Bizare, stayed on with me as an MGA, and I'd actually built a good relationship with the PR guy after our initial issue with his "leads." As our camaraderie improved, we divided up the work and we were humming. Phil handled all of the training, and I promoted another guy to help manage the office. As we began to improve the quality of our leads, we were able to recruit better and we all prospered.

In what felt like no time, I had three Master General

Agents, eight General Agents, and dozens of agents. I soon realized that we'd need a lot more space than the Des Plaines office and the Teamster Hall office, so I found us a building downtown on Wacker Drive that was really nice.

The building was free standing, but it was very close to other buildings, so you couldn't tell how big it really was. From the outside it was deceptive, but we had the whole floor to ourselves, and it was a really impressive space. My office overlooked the river, and I had a glass bottle desk with fluorescent lights in it. At the time we were investing a lot of money in our offices because we wanted them to look sharp so we could recruit in the cities. As it was, it was hard enough to get talented people from the suburbs to come in, so we needed a little home field advantage. In hindsight, it was probably too extravagant and cost too much.

In addition to the business move, I made a personal move as well. I took Dottie, who was pregnant with our son Adam, and our daughter Emily to a really nice two-story house in River Forest, a suburb outside the city. To give you an idea of how casually (and how often) the mob was brought up in conversation, when we were house hunting our real estate agent mentioned that one of the big mafia families lived a block or so away—and that was a really big bonus because it kept the area safe! Her implication was that nobody was going to mess around in a neighborhood with a mob boss sleeping a few doors down. I laugh about that to this day. It was all so commonplace there.

The only downside to the house was that the drive into Chicago could be an hour depending on the traffic. The freeway was always backed up. I took shortcuts through West Chicago, and that area looked like a bombed-out third-world country back then. Everything was boarded up. I remember a female agent once went to do a presentation in that area and came out to find a bullet in her radiator. After that she told me it wasn't safe to go there. I told her she could handle it and offered to go with her the next day to give presentations in the area. Well, the next day we went, and we were standing on the steps of a building waiting for an appointment. When they came home, the man had his arm in a sling. He told us that he was standing right where we were and that he'd been shot in a drive-by. Needless to say, I pulled that agent out of that neighborhood! As for my commute, I knew it was a little dangerous, but it could save me twenty minutes every morning, so I did it anyway.

I was still big into motivational tapes then, so I'd listen to them on my drive to work. I tried audiobooks for a while, but I'd start to listen and then my mind would wander to something else, and in five minutes I'd lost my place in the book.

I really enjoyed the scenery in Chicago and the town as a whole. I was also fortunate enough to get to do some of the classic "Chicago" things like attend games and concerts and other events. I wasn't a big sports fan, but I did go to Soldier Field for a Bears game that first winter, and it was the absolute coldest experience of my life. I thought I was going to freeze to death and ended up spending a majority of the game standing by a heater. It felt like someone had invited me to the Arctic Circle to watch football—not my cup of tea.

Aside from that little escapade, there were so many great restaurants in the city to enjoy, and we were always throwing company contests in which we gave away steak dinners, along with Bulls and Cubs and White Sox tickets. It was a good town with lots of stuff to do, and it suited me.

For the first time in my life, I was having success and my mind wasn't a drug-addled mess, so I could actually enjoy the process and plot methodically ahead to my next moves. For me, that included aggressively expanding beyond my Wacker Drive office and the other two offices around Chicago. Over the next few years, I opened offices in Peoria, Springfield, and Decatur. I also started pushing west into Iowa with an office in Quad Cities, and east into Indiana with offices in Hammond and Gary. Before

I knew it, I was in charge of a giant territory that spanned three states.

Of course, Mr. Rapoport had to approve each move into a new territory, but as an SGA I was allowed to have a presence in up to three states, so that's what I did. If I thought a guy near me in Indiana or Iowa wasn't doing well, I'd ask to take over. After it was approved, I just had to negotiate whether or not I'd buy the furniture, and then I changed the lease for the office space over to my name. After that, all the assets were under my control.

The office in Chicago was by far the costliest operation I had. In fact, it was finding inexpensive office space in the smaller cities where the profit margin was much higher that funded the main hub. Those smaller offices really were your profit centers, and the more of those you had, the more revenue you could derive from your territory.

It took about a year and a half to have a fully mature new office. First, you had to promote an MGA from an already well-run office to take over the new office. Then, you had to give him time to recruit new people and groom enough of them to the Supervising Agent and General Agent levels. Once you had enough of those guys in place and they were hitting their numbers, then you could consider that office a success and think about expanding again.

My great Midwest expansion lasted almost a full

decade, from 1986 to 1996. The population of Chicago was so big and the unions were so strong that I was able to continue to surpass my quotas in the city while also growing the satellite territories. Really, as the unions organized and increased their membership, we were able to meet with them, and once our relationship was rock solid, the unions became de facto funnels for new clients. The more members they organized, the more people we'd be able to make our pitch to. As my territory grew larger, I became one of the more influential SGAs at American Income. But my ambition at that time stayed largely in that city. In fact, I may have stayed there for the long haul and continued to eat up territory if not for a catastrophe that nearly ended my life.

One minute I'm riding my motorcycle down the highway, and the next I wake up in excruciating pain in the hospital, barely able to move. In my mind, that's essentially how the accident went down. In reality, I was cruising down the road on my bike and was hit by a car so hard that I *flew over the car* and my body smashed into the ground. I broke my arm in nine places, shattered my collarbone, and had heavy bruises and scrapes all over my body. I even severed the radial nerve in my right arm.

I was lucky to be alive, and God was clearly watching over me on this one!

Normally, I'm not one to grasp onto clichés, but I have to say that the one about how near-death experiences change your life is true. I say this, because after that accident, while I was lying in the hospital bed with a cast covering my whole right side, I had plenty of time to think about my life up that point. Emotionally, I was shaken that I almost died; physically, I was scared that I might not regain the use of my right arm or that I may have to live in chronic pain or... everything, really. Your mind wanders to dark places after things like that happen.

On a personal level, I thought a lot about my family and how my position in Chicago, along with my responsibilities to the company and the union, kept me away from my wife and kids a majority of the time. I had that moment of truth when I thought, *what am I doing?* and *what is life all about?*

Here I was, lucky enough to have overcome severe alcohol and drug addictions, and I'd been blessed with a second chance at a lucrative career that I almost threw away. I've got a wife and kids...and all I do is work.

I thought, *I spend no quality time with my kids. I spend little quality time with my wife. I don't set aside any time to take care of myself and enjoy life. What the hell am I doing with myself?*

During one of these inner monologues in the hospital, I hatched the idea that I was going to give up the big city life, take a step back, and really focus on things that were important to me: my family and my well-being. Specifically, I decided then and there that I was going to begin planning to leave the Chicago office and the center of the labor movement and the enormous territory I'd amassed (and the miserable winters), and I was going to move my family to a nice place on the beach in South Carolina.

To me, the plan felt terrific and was the perfect elixir. The more I thought about it, the better it all felt: I'd leave Chicago, take over a small territory in a small state, lighten my workload, be home, enjoy my children and the ocean and the fresh air, and really, truly, finally enjoy my life.

But first, I had to recover.

Once the swelling went down all over my body and it looked like my collarbone was going to heal just fine, the focus of the rehab went to my right arm. When I left the hospital I had a pretty serious cast on my arm and shoulder. The cast kept my arm stretched out, and I really couldn't open and close my hand. I was in my forties at this point, so I wasn't a young guy, and the healing took forever. I also needed multiple surgeries on my arm over time to improve my range of motion and hopefully give me use of the whole limb.

I had a real tough time doing a lot of normal things during my recovery period. I needed my wife to help me get dressed and even put on my underwear. One time she was helping me get my underwear on and the doorbell rang. She went to answer the door and I was completely stuck. I stayed in that position with my underwear around my ankles for about fifteen minutes, and man, I was fuming. At the time I'd been slacking on the rehab a little, but no more. After being stuck with my Fruit of the Looms by my feet, I committed 100% to getting my body back to normal.

Another situation that I can laugh about now, but at the time wasn't very funny, came a little later in my recovery process. I was having new carpet installed in an office I was working in, and I was told it was done. I opened the door to check it out, and just like in a cartoon, the carpet slid right out from under me, and I slammed onto the ground flat on my back. Not only did the fall knock loose one of the stabilizing pipes that ran down my shoulder into my arm in the cast, but because the glue under the carpet hadn't dried, my entire backside was covered in high-grade carpenter glue that could dry at any minute.

I was in searing pain, and I had a vision of my clothes becoming super glued to the back of my body. I don't

THE CHICAGO COMEBACK, 1986

even know how they would go about getting clothes off at that point, so before it dried, I took off my clothes as best I could and had my secretary run to the store to get me a new set of clothes to wear. I laugh about it now just describing it, but the fall ended up being a big setback because I re-injured my arm.

Eventually, I recovered enough to begin to execute my plan to slow my life down and move to South Carolina.

CHAPTER 12

South Carolina, 1996

From my small apartment in Columbia, South Carolina, I moved the chess pieces around to set up my new southern, laid-back life. My wife and I decided it would be best if she and the kids stayed in Chicago while I got things squared away, so for about six months I travelled back and forth between South Carolina and Chicago. The place I had in Columbia was nothing special, but I dug the southern hospitality, and the change of pace from the frenzied lifestyle of the Windy City was refreshing.

Using Columbia as my main hub, I also opened up offices in Greenville and Charleston, where I had another executive apartment for a short period of time. Charleston was a wonderful town right on the water, and it had such a quintessential southern feel. It had great barbecue, and the blue-green water that meandered in and out of the inlets and rivers and estuaries was beautiful. I even liked the mix of colonial and classical architecture around the city.

Once I had my satellite offices in place and I'd put the right people in the right cities, my wife and my two kids, Emily and Adam, joined me. We decided to buy a nice piece of property on Pawleys Island, about forty minutes south of Myrtle Beach. That was such a terrific area. I remember driving up to our property from Charleston and seeing thousands of pine trees that looked like giant rows of pencils. There were no branches or anything on them, and I remember thinking, *Man, I didn't know beavers could climb trees.* But the trees hadn't been chewed on by beavers; they'd been demolished by Hurricane Hugo a few years before.

In any case, the land we bought on Pawleys Island had previously been the site of a bed and breakfast that was washed away by Hugo. It was right on the water and was the perfect beach location for a house. Since the bed and breakfast was gone, the only thing left was a little guest house, and that's where we lived while we constructed the main house as an extension of the guest house. When it was finished, the main house and the existing house were about 4,000 square feet in total. It was nothing extravagant, and we built it with more of a modern architecture style. We had giant, portrait windows installed throughout the house. The locals thought we were nuts. This was before builders began using impact glass for houses in hurricane zones, so those giant windows were like a bulls-eye for hurricane winds. Truth be told the windows were never destroyed, but we were evacuated two or three times a year while we lived there, so I guess we got lucky.

With the construction of my house underway, and my wife and kids happy to be out of Chicago and on the beach, I set about getting used to this new life I thought I wanted so much. Yes, the pace of life was slower, and yes, the people were calmer, and the geography was beautiful, and I truly loved the ocean—but in the end, I was still me. Even though I told myself that I should take it easy and stay home with the kids and enjoy the life I'd dreamt about while in the hospital, within a few short months I was back on the road all the time.

South Carolina was obviously a much less population-dense territory, but I still had offices all over the state to visit, so I was always driving out to Greenville or back to Columbia, or out to another place. Basically, I was running around just as I had in Chicago. The biggest difference was that I wasn't in a top-five major metro area of the United States. From a city and population standpoint, I went from the Major Leagues to low-level minor league ball.

And I have to reiterate that I really, honestly thought

that was what I needed and wanted at the time. But I was fooling myself. South Carolina was so small and so far away from the big action that it was boring to me. I felt like I couldn't have an impact on the company. If I had a monster quarter in Chicago, people took notice and it moved American Income's bottom line. Everything in South Carolina felt like a whimper. There was no excitement. No adrenaline. I sorely missed that feeling of walking into a huge office in a huge city and firing up my crew. I missed being in expansion mode. Basically, I got what I thought I wanted but I wasn't happy at all.

My family, however, *was* happy. They really enjoyed being on Pawleys Island, which I understood. If I were a little kid, I'd love to live on the beach and not having winter too. But after about two years, I was dying on the inside and knew I had to make a move. Once again, I called Mr. Rapoport to discuss my options with the company and we came up with a big idea.

Let's open up New York State.

New York State was a labyrinth of insurance rules and regulations, and up to that point, American Income Life hadn't taken a foothold there. In order to "open it up," as we said, we were going to have to literally open up a separate insurance company as a subsidiary of AIL. There was an incredible amount of red tape, and if we were going to go all in we'd have to pull off some legal gymnastics to make it work.

The more we talked, the more excited we got about the idea. Because I had a lot of success in Chicago, I had the right background and experience to lead the charge in New York. As the move slowly became a reality, I got my wife on board, and we slowly began to prepare the kids for a serious change of scenery: the lazy beaches of South Carolina for New York City. They were young at the time, but it was still going to be an adjustment, so we talked a lot about how great the city was. We told the kids about the skyscrapers and the parks and the culture and the food and the plays and the pizza—anything to get them excited about the move.

The time finally came for me to fly to Waco to discuss the preparations for New York City with Mr. Rapoport. However, my life ended up changing in an entirely different and unexpected way.

In order to explain exactly what happened to me during these few frenetic weeks of my life, a little context about American Income at that time is necessary.

In 1980, Liberty National acquired Globe Life and Accident Insurance Company and formed the holding company Torchmark Corporation. Over the ensuing decades, Torchmark began acquiring more and more insurance companies, including United Investors Life Insurance and Waddell and Reed Financial. Then in 1994, Torchmark bought American Income Life, and for several years it was a great deal. AIL was growing consistently, and then all of a sudden around 1996 it stopped growing.

Part of the reason for this was that many of the top-level executives at AIL stopped thinking about the company's future to focus on their own. Mr. Rapoport was butting heads with the president of the company, Chuck Cooper, and they were constantly maneuvering behind each other's backs and sabotaging each other to wrest control of the company. While they angled for power plays against each other, the company's bottom line remained flat for several years. It was as if they were so focused on pulling a coup on the other guy that they forgot there was an actual company to run. This created a lot of uncertainty, and it trickled down the whole company. Productivity suffered from top-to-bottom.

All of this came to a head when CB Hudson, the CEO of Torchmark, was asked on an analysts call about why American Income had stopped growing. Hudson gave a few reasons, and somewhere in his answer said, "If the stagnation continues, they'll have to make some changes at the top of management."

Mr. Rapoport went absolutely berserk and began plotting his revenge and next moves. It was during this time that he agreed to the big idea to open up New York City with me. Being in South Carolina at the time, I wasn't aware of how bad the blood was between the executives at American Income. I just thought I was talking to Mr. Rapoport about opening up New York City.

Right before I was to fly down to meet with Mr. Rapoport, I got a call from company president Chuck Cooper. "Listen, I know you're coming to look at New York, but I'd like you to look at coming into the home office to help me run the company."

This was a surprising turn of events for me because I didn't know who had the authority to do what, but I could tell there was a lot of triangulating going on between Cooper, Mr. Rapoport, and another executive, Bill Garner. Basically, in the week leading up to my New York City discussion, Mr. Rapoport exploded about the analysts call, and it looked like he was either going to be fired or leave the company. Cooper, who had been maneuvering behind the scenes this whole time, thought he was a shoo-in to take over the company. He figured if he had me on board, as one of Mr. Rapoport's proteges, it would solidify his power grab and he could then fire Bill Garner, leaving just Cooper and me to run the company.

Cooper overplayed his hand.

When I arrived in Waco, Mr. Rapoport decided to "retire," and I ended up interviewing with Torchmark CEO CB Hudson and one of his top guys, Mark McAndrew, for the Executive Vice President job with American Income Life. While I was interviewing and discussing the steps to become the Executive VP, Cooper was throwing his weight around and causing trouble for Hudson and McAndrew. He eventually gave them an ultimatum.

He lost.

Hudson fired Cooper, installed McAndrew as the President and CEO, and made me the Executive Vice President.

What a whirlwind!

Inside of three months I'd convinced my family to move to New York City so I could be the new SGA there, and then all of a sudden we were moving to Waco, Texas so I could be an executive in the company. It was a head trip for me, and I felt awful because I'd spent all this time selling the kids on the wonders of New York City. Now, they were moving from the beach in South Carolina to the home of David Koresh. Obviously, this was a really hard sell.

This was an incredible turn of events in my life, and

it changed everything for me. I'd gone from being a chess piece in the company to one of the main players, and it really opened up my mind as to how high I could climb. But first, I had to figure out what the hell an Executive Vice President did!

CHAPTER 13

A Brief Stop in Dallas, 1999

The kids got used to living on the water in South Carolina, so I tried to ease the transition to Dallas by getting us a place in Rockwall, on Lake Ray Hubbard. It wasn't the ocean, but it wasn't the city, either. The house was right next to the marina, and it was nice. But if you left any lights on at night, the screens everywhere got covered with bugs. The area around the lake was unlike most of the other suburbs of Dallas. We didn't have waves and surf anymore, but there was a big fishing and boating culture that most people who've never been to the area didn't know about.

The house was forty minutes south of Torchmark's home office in McKinney, where I was going to train directly under Mark McAndrew, who would quickly become one of my mentors. Mark had a brilliant analytical mind. He could process and solve the most complex company-wide issues in a matter of hours, whereas it would take me three days to sit down and figure out what was going on. He had two favorite sayings that have stuck with me to this day.

The first was, "Nothing is as good as it seems, and nothing is as bad as it seems."

The second was, "Respond, don't react."

I have found more and more wisdom in these words as the years have gone by.

Mark was also very adept at navigating the politics of a big corporation. I was very fortunate when I joined the home office because he sheltered me from all of that. He basically said, "Go do your thing. I'll take care of all this other stuff."

It didn't take long for me to realize why CB Hudson had paired us together. While I'd spent my career at AIL building workforces all over the country and rallying the troops to my cause, Mark had a more introverted demeanor. The overall culture was one where corporate executives would walk down the hallway and not even say hello to anyone. It was quiet as a library. They didn't have the kind of guys in place to energize an organization.

It was hard for me to believe it, but when I looked in the mirror, I saw that I actually *was* that kind of guy— at least from an experience perspective. From an executive perspective, I was as green as they came. I remember buying John Maxwell's book, *The 21 Irrefutable Laws of Leadership* to prepare myself to run the company. After I finished it I had to laugh: I was 0-21 on following his laws!

When it came to some of his more well-known laws, like the one on transformative leadership that states your best growth comes from helping others grow, I hadn't spent much time thinking about that, other than on a quota level. Or his "law of the lid" that states you are not master of all and you can't do everything by yourself, I had to really dig into that one. I was used to running a territory and pulling every single lever that needed to be pulled. Now that I was in the home office, there was no way I could do that. I was going to have to put systems in place and let the people do their thing.

As I read the list one-by-one, I came to the conclusion that I was going to have to transform myself to be the leader that I knew I could be.

Another issue I found myself obsessing over was the fact that I barely attended high school or college. I couldn't get out of my head that I was going to be an executive at a large company and I didn't have a business school background. I didn't have an MBA; I had a GED. I hadn't worked as an executive at another company. I didn't have any kind of financial background.

When I was lying in bed at night I often thought, *Jeez, I don't know if I have any of the skill sets necessary to make this work.* Believe me, I had a real inferiority complex when it came to my lack of a college education. The more I got involved on the financial side, we'd sit in meetings and go over profit and loss statements and EBITDA and projections and run rates and spreadsheets...my brain would often feel like it was going to explode. I'd look around at the other executives who spoke this "financial language," and I'd be jealous in a way. I felt like a kid in a grade school classroom who couldn't read. I understood that I was going to have to work harder than everybody else to excel.

The one thing I did have going for me, however, was that I flat out knew how to run an agency from the ground up. I'd held every single position inside an agency, and I knew every job inside and out. Not only that, but I'd run these agencies and learned these jobs all over the country, from the Pacific to the South to the Midwest and the Mid-Atlantic. I knew the particular issues each territory faced better than anyone in the company, and certainly better than anyone in a corporate boardroom. Nobody could bullshit me about why something on the ground was or wasn't working.

That was my key strength, and I leaned on it as much as I could. I knew exactly what an SGA needed to do to be successful, and I knew that the company's success (and mine as an executive) relied on having successful SGAs. When I looked at things from that vantage point, I realized that *I can do this*. I just needed to extrapolate what I'd learned at the SGA level and take it up to the corporate level.

The last issue to overcome was the inevitable jealousies and doubts from my colleagues. A lot of the SGAs all over the country were my friends, and now I was going to be their boss. I knew that pissed a lot of them off because several of the guys in bigger territories thought they should have gotten the executive vice president job. Looking back, I think I was in a unique position to be chosen. A lot of the SGAs had created bad blood over the years through their tactics or their attitudes, or maybe just their abrasive personalities. I didn't really have any enemies in the company, and there were a lot of guys I'd helped train over the years who had a lot of success.

Still, there was no shortage of people who doubted me!

After about nine months in the McKinney office, several things occurred to me, and I acted quickly.

The first was that Mark McAndrew had his sights on becoming the Torchmark CEO one day, which meant that I had a direct line of sight to becoming President and CEO of American Income Life, and that's what I wanted.

Second, if I was going to enact any real change and grow the company, I firmly believed I couldn't do it from McKinney. I had to be sitting in with everybody at the home office and voicing my opinion on where we needed to go.

Also, the home office at that time was a hotbed of mass confusion. Nobody knew what was going to happen with their jobs or the unions. It was clear that they needed me on the ground in Waco to provide stability.

PART IV

AT THE HELM

CHAPTER 14

Time to Run the Company Waco, Texas, 2000

When I took over as Executive Vice President, American Income Life was a $46 million company. Mr. Rapoport was never able to cross the $50 million barrier, but when I began running things, one of the first goals I had in mind was to make us a $100 million dollar company. That was where I wanted to go, and in order to do that I reviewed every single company policy and strategy and put it on trial.

My basic question with everything, from hiring to promoting to training and presentations, was:

Why do we do this?

If the answer was, "Because that's the way we've always done it," then I immediately put it under a microscope to decide whether I should keep it, fix it, or toss it. My goal was to develop new strategies that would lead to growth and get rid of anything internal that might stand in the way.

But there was no way I could do this alone!

I needed really smart, creative leaders who I could trust to help get the company to where it needed to be. One of the most important people to our success was Debbie Gamble, the Senior Vice President of Agency. She was the liaison between the agency force and the SGAs, and the home office and the executives. She and her team were the ones that were constantly on the phone with the SGAs. If there was a problem, they were calling her. It could be about anything—advances, agents, office issues, whatever.

I loved working with her because she was the type of person who asked smart questions that would force me and others to really think things through.

During my first week she was pelting me with questions: "What do you want to do about this? What do you want to do about that? How do you want to handle this?"

I remember saying, "Just do what you do for now and let me catch up a bit."

But really, I was procrastinating, and she forced me to think by continuing to ask me really smart questions. And these weren't just yes or no things. She was great at figuring out the cause and effect of ideas before you'd implement them.

If you do this, this may happen, so how do you want to handle that?

Without that person, you can't move forward on this project.

Without someone like Debbie on our team, we'd have spent all our time putting out fires. Debbie was so crucial to our organization, and she helped me do away with so many inefficiencies.

A good example of this was an aptitude test for new hires that someone in the company had instituted. Basically, it said that if you were running an agency, you couldn't hire anybody who failed this test. But what was the test looking for? What did we learn about potential hires from this test? How were we measuring whether this test was effective?

The answer to all of the above questions, and almost anything having to do with this dumb test, was, "We don't know."

Most of the SGAs we had likely wouldn't have passed the test when they first joined the company, and I'm pretty sure I wouldn't have either. After asking around about where the test came from and why it was used, the only feedback I got was that the test was holding back recruiting and preventing us from making promising hires. Someone said that it was there to help with coaching or some nonsense like that, but to me it was pretty clear that this test accomplished only two things. One, it hurt our recruitment, and two, it was making this testing company a lot of money without any accountability. Obviously, neither of these things were beneficial to American Income, so I dropped that test from the company right away.

That was low-hanging fruit, so to speak, because there weren't many people who were fighting to keep the test. It was a quick win, but it gave me some momentum.

Another area of the company I needed to learn more about to secure our successful future was our presence in Washington, D.C.

We had a gentleman working there by the name of Jules Pagano who dealt with the international union presidents. When I was an SGA, I mostly saw him trailing Mr. Rapoport wherever he went, so I thought he was just another gopher. Boy, was I wrong! When I began to learn about how our relationship with D.C. worked, I realized that Pagano was extremely important. The respect that the labor leaders had for him was eye opening. It was on another level.

In this D.C. office there were fifty-three international or past international union presidents who sat on our Labor Advisory Board. They'd help us get the locals within their own union, and they'd advise us on all other kinds of matters. I'd often find myself in meetings with Pagano and these old, retired guys, and I'd ask why we needed to meet them. , "These are the guys who have the knowledge that can help us," Pagano would say.

He knew everyone, and he was invaluable. He allowed us to have instant credibility with a union. For instance, when my PR person went to the bricklayers union, she'd go through her presentation and show them the picture of our Labor Advisory Board, and she'd say, "and here's your International Union President on our board."

That was huge. Once I got started, I was in D.C. a minimum of once a month to make sure I had meetings with these international presidents. Eventually, I asked Denise Boyer if she would move to D.C. to help Jules Pagano. She was a union organizer before she came to American Income. Her job was to help Pagano be more involved in the progressive movement of things. That solidified our presence, and it was critical to growing the company.

Moving Denise to D.C. was a smart move that got no resistance. Again, just like getting rid of that test, it was a simple win to keep our early momentum.

Most of the changes we began making after that got much more pushback and required a more creative—and sometimes heavy-handed—approach. In order to implement this new vision we had for the company, we created the Executive Sales Team. This was a group of people who implemented all of the ideas that we came up with.

To my mind, a leader is a visionary who rallies a team to create new systems for growth—and you need people who can implement these systems. That was the Executive Sales Team. As we were starting to grow the company, Scott Smith, Bob Falvo, and Domenico Bertini became keys to our success.

In addition to the directors, that was the team in charge of implementing our vision and making it come true on the sales side. They were collectively in charge of ensuring that anything we mandated from the home office was being applied in the field. Scott had the job of promoting SGAs, and on the flipside, he was in charge of demoting guys if they weren't getting in line or performing. With the Executive Sales Team in line, things could really get moving.

Together, my team and I came back with five game changers that we felt could get us past that $100 million mark.

CHAPTER 15

Game Changers

American Income Life was only as strong as its State General Agents, which meant that the key to growth in the company was having a stacked pipeline of RGAs (a new level of contract that was added because of the growth of the bigger agencies) and Master General Agents who could be future SGAs. This sounds simple and obvious, but the system we inherited actually managed to have the opposite effect. Due to the way the company paid its contractors and rewarded production and renewals, SGAs actually found themselves in a position where it was in their best interest to never let their top MGAs leave their hierarchy. It was backwards and it really contributed to the flatlining of the business.

For example, if an SGA had a really talented MGA that was ready to be promoted, it was actually better business for the SGA to keep the MGA under him and not help him advance. Why? Because by keeping the MGA under him, he would keep the MGA's business and production. Remember, all of our agents were independent contractors, and an SGA was essentially running his own agency under the American Income banner. This created a situation where the guy running the company (me) was pulling in a different direction than the person the MGA was loyal to (the SGA), even though I'm the one trying to promote the MGA.

See? Backwards.

This also created an issue where a talented MGA was likely isolated from the rest of the company. If they were sheltered by their SGA, they really had no idea of what the possibilities for advancement were. The person in charge of sharing that information—the SGA—may have downplayed corporate, or worse, talked poorly about us to keep his MGA in place.

It's a little confusing, I know, but what it often boiled down to was a tug-of-war between American Income executives and an SGA, with the MGA in the middle. Making matters more difficult, some SGAs were offering partnerships to their biggest MGAs, which completely stalled our talent pool. This had been going on for years, and it was one of the big reasons we weren't growing. A lot of our talent was stuck in one place, and the MGAs were loyal to the

SGAs and not the company at-large. This bottleneck was suffocating our company, and it actually went all the way down the agent chain. In the end, it was a combination of partnerships and independent SGAs that equaled the perfect equation for growing the SGA body. At the time, however, we didn't know that yet.

If we weren't promoting our supervising agents, and we weren't building up the management team because a glut of SGAs were keeping their best agents in the same spot, then it didn't matter how well we recruited because there was a choke point that stopped the talent from going any higher. The reality is that someone is going to lead eight to ten people really well, but they may not lead twenty people really well, so you needed more people who could lead eight to ten agents. That's how you build strong agencies. We needed to grow leadership at all levels with incentives built in for them to grow and promote their guys.

The simplest way to tackle this problem was to, in a way, throw money at it. Of course, I'm not talking about haphazardly wasting money. Rather, if we wanted General Agents to build their teams, we'd put together a bonus structure that financially rewarded the building of a team.

This was an approach that we constantly had to tweak. Occasionally, you'd over-incentivize something to the detriment of something else. One year we decided to pull some money from the MGA bonuses and give it to the Supervising Agents. Boy, was that a bad idea. We saved some money, but we lost or ticked off so many MGAs that it really put us in a bind. The MGAs were the lifeblood to our growth, so we had to reverse course. But that was how I saw my job. I was always rocking the boat, challenging the status quo of what was going on. I was never afraid to try things, and I was never afraid to make corrections if the idea was a flop.

Eventually, one of the ways we solved the tug-of-war to promote MGAs was to offer the SGAs incentives for grooming future leadership. When it came to building what I eventually would call my "bullpen,"—agents who I believed had the talent to become SGAs—I turned to the leadership school we ran from the home office. When I got there, there were people who were teaching classes on sales and presenting and managing that were at the bottom in terms of production.

Let me tell you, you don't want someone who isn't successful teaching a class. I overhauled that whole process and got some of our best talent to teach the classes. I also tightened up who could attend. I wanted people who had been with the company for at least six months, and I wanted the SGAs to have skin in the game. I made it so the SGAs paid for their agents to attend, and they nominated the agents as well.

The agents would then fly to us for a week, which was great from two perspectives. From my perspective, I got to meet (or at least have people who I trusted meet) some of the young talent we had in the company. And since I'd put those rules in place, these were agents who were likely to stick around and who had the seal of approval from their SGAs.

From the agent's perspective, it gave them a chance to really see the size and scope of the company. Up to that point, their whole world in terms of American Income was likely just their agency. Now they got to see that they were a part of something much bigger and that their future might take them beyond the city they were in. This was critical when it came to building the bullpen I mentioned. When agents were at the leadership school, we planted the seed in them that they could go as high as their work ethic and ambition would take them.

As the agents worked their way up, the classes went from fifty to seventy people per class to much smaller groups, until it got down to ten to twelve people who were the high-level MGAs. This was the end of my bullpen funnel, and these were the agents who I saw as the future of American Income. Once we unclogged the talent pipeline with a mix of these initiatives, the company was back in position to grow.

The final piece to this puzzle was to take a long, hard look at how each SGA was performing. There was a lot of complacency and stagnation throughout the company, so if a guy was flat and wasn't improving, we'd have a discussion about what was expected under my regime. I'd typically give an SGA ninety days to turn things around, but I could tell right away who was going to keep doing things their way and who would embrace what I was telling them.

Another strategy we employed much later on, once we controlled the lead source (which I'll get to next), was to move a strong SGA into a weaker SGA's territory. This was obviously not very popular among many SGAs. What SGA would want another SGA right there? None. But in order to do it effectively, we needed to make another drastic change.

———

As I've written about all of my moves and described how I built agencies in several states, I've made a point to discuss how critical the public relations team was to each territory. Everything I wrote about public relations to this point was from the perspective of an SGA because that was my perspective and it was my reality. During my ascent with American Income, I thought of public relations only from my territory's perspective. Now that I was an executive, I began to think about how limiting it could be for the growth of the company to have individual public relations teams for each agency.

You may remember that when I'd take over a new territory, I'd have to buy the leads from the existing SGA? Well, this practice had gone on for the entire history of the company, and while it was effective on a local level for generating actual leads, when it came to running the company and being nimble with our management, it was a mess and actually stifled movement.

For instance, if I wanted to move agents around or have them switch territories, the SGAs still had control of their leads, and I had no access to them. Usually, if I'm moving one guy into a territory it means I'm moving another guy out, and typically, the guy being moved out isn't thrilled about it. Consequently, he may not be very cooperative or timely when it came to sharing his leads. Also, that particular SGA owned them, so they looked at their leads as equity to be sold.

From that standpoint, the way things were set up made no sense. Why should the executives at American Income be held hostage (from a leads standpoint) by the SGAs? What this arrangement effectively created was a scenario in which the SGA had the control of a territory, not American Income. It was an unnecessary obstacle to managing the company that we didn't need, so we came up with a solution that was a radical change for the company: We centralized PR.

This was a seismic shift in how we did business, and we could not have done it without some great leaders in the company. In particular,

Diana Crosby, who was the Head of Policy Owner Service, took over the transitional part of the PR centralization and did a phenomenal job. She was in charge of the company-wide lead generation and became the hub of the whole operation. We also brought in Debbie Enstedt, the Vice President of Public Relations, to be in charge of field operations for PR.

They worked hand-in-hand to make sure all of the changes we made to our PR strategy trickled down efficiently and effectively throughout the company.

Words like "system" and "organization" did not come as second nature to me. I came from sales. Those things certainly weren't my strong suits. But Diana was tremendous! She put the whole formulation together, from the systems to the data to everything else.

After she took over, instead of SGAs being responsible for generating leads and paying PR staff, we took it over at the home office. And let me tell you, we got a lot of pushback on this!

There were plenty of SGAs who would have kicked me right out of the company if they could have! It was such a battle because it was about control and ego. If the home office owned the leads, then we could set a formula and charge the same amount per lead to everyone. Well, there were maybe ten SGAs who did a really good job with PR, so they hated this arrangement. But I firmly believed this was one of those battles I had to wage as a leader because the new system was going to work better on so many levels.

When it came to our management pipeline, MGAs didn't even learn about public relations until they became SGAs. There was no training until they actually had the SGA position, so there was a learning curve to that, and it added to the workload a new SGA was facing. It was also intimidating and may have prevented some MGAs from pursuing a higher position. After all, who wants to deal with the headache of PR if you don't have to?

Also, prior to American Income controlling the leads, we had to start from scratch every time we replaced an SGA. The new SGA was in charge of generating his own leads, and the territory was in his hands alone. From an executive standpoint, all we could do was hope that the new agent would do better. By switching things so American Income controlled the leads, we could put several SGAs into an area and hand out the leads as needed. We could

THE MOST UNLIKELY LEADER

have one SGA who was flat, another who was growing, and another who was learning the ropes, and they could all be in a major area like Illinois.

As a leader of the company, this gave me options with my territories that I didn't have before, and it allowed me to look at the company as a whole as if it were a chessboard. I could move the pieces around much more easily and with as little friction as possible from a mechanics standpoint. Yes, some SGAs weren't happy about it because they'd been doing PR on their own for so long, and yes, others weren't happy about it because I could easily put someone right in their backyard for competition if they weren't doing their jobs. But that's business! When you sign an SGA contract you take on the responsibility of growth.

I also found that the new crop of SGAs really liked the arrangement. For them, public relations was something they'd never handled, but they knew it was important. Now when they got a big promotion, they learned that the home office was going to take PR off their plate. They liked that.

The key to making all of this work was that Diana Crosby had to create an in-house public relations staff that reported to the home office. Up to that point, our PR people were independent contractors, and since we were asking them to work for American Income and not a local SGA, we believed they should be American Income employees with benefits like health insurance and a 401k. To do this, we created a vertical hierarchy of public relations people throughout the United States. We took four or five of our best public relations people and made them Public Relations Directors in different regions all over the country. Each director was leading a team of Public Relations Managers, who oversaw the territories in their region, and then each manager was in charge of a smaller team of four or five people on the ground.

A few of the older public relations people stayed on in this hierarchy as independent contractors, and that was fine. Within a couple years, nearly 100% of the corporate public relations team were employees, and the strategy worked perfectly. Not only were SGAs moving around more freely and we were able to bump up the right MGAs, but our potential to grow increased exponentially.

———

The last problem to fix from an SGA perspective was how we handled advances. For this, I have to give credit to Mark McAndrew, who modeled our new system after that of our sister company, United American Insurance.

Without getting into too many details, the system when we took over involved American Income Life loaning money to an SGA because there was no way he could pay all of his expenses on his earned income alone. Since the SGA needed to spread out the money, he'd put a lot of these expenses on his MGAs. So now the MGA, who had fewer renewals and less income, was getting dumped on. Then, if that MGA was ready to become an SGA, we'd look at his financials and find out that he was already $100,000 in debt to the company before he even started his business.

One of the first things we did away with was the MGA charges. We put a rule in place that stated an SGA couldn't charge an MGA for any expenses. So when an MGA was ready to start his own territory, he could start with a clean slate.

McAndrew also came up with the idea to designate all advanced money paid from the agent level to the SGA level as taxable income. There would be no more interest charged on the debit balance.

This was a brilliant move by McAndrew. It cleaned up our books and paved the way for more streamlined MGA advancement.

It took a long time to get everyone to buy in to our centralized public relations team, but in the meantime we wanted to get past another hurdle: the number of referrals we were getting. For the majority of my career, the company focused mostly on union leads. I'd say over 80% of the business was union-based. It had been a good strategy and helped build a sound company and reputation, but I believed that working solely with union leads was one of the big reasons why the company never recorded a $50 million year. I believed in my heart that we could get to $250 million, but we needed to expand our base of referrals drastically. After all, if a lead was warm because it came with an endorsement from a union, it was even warmer if it came from a trusted friend and someone who recently purchased insurance from American Income.

I had a friend in New Jersey who was having a ton of success working referrals, so I flew him in and he gave me a demonstration. I'll never forget it. We set up four appointments on a New Year's Eve, we went into four homes, and we walked away with forty new leads. It was a real eye opener for me, and once I was running the company, I mandated that getting referrals was part of every presentation.

That put us in a scenario where we'd have the policyholders as a lead, then we'd get referrals off the policyholders, and that expanded our lead base. All of a sudden, we had another 30% of our business coming from referrals, and that number continued to grow. Then we'd wait a year and call back the policyholder to ask them about updating their policy and offer new products, and that gave us a higher persistency rate.

All of these changes begat new changes. Mark and I liked to test things out in different areas of the company. We'd run A tests, B tests, C tests, and D tests on everything, from recruiting to referrals. If we saw a strategy that worked or we thought of a new strategy, we'd test it. If it worked in one test and then another, we'd expand it even more. This way, when we approached an SGA or a group of SGAs about a change and they had objections, we could defend the changes with hard data from real-world trials.

———————

While we were discussing the addition of referrals to the presentation, we began to think bigger:

What if the whole company ran off one presentation?

As things stood back then, every SGA had his own version of the company presentation and he trained all of his agents his way.

Why didn't we have everyone on the same presentation?

Well, the answer was that it was one of those, "because that's the way we've always done it" situations that I hated. As far as I could gather, the reason everyone was on a different presentation was because nobody had tried to get the whole company on the same one. Simple explanation. The difficulty came with what to do with that information.

When I began to think about things from a company standpoint, it occurred to me that one of the biggest variables we had when it came to measuring an agent's success was their presentation. Given two SGAs with equal talent and work ethic and management skill, the one with the better presentation would produce more business with his agency. That's basic logic. But as things stood, we had no way to be sure everyone was running off the most effective presentation. I hated being in the dark when it came to data, so I needed a way to standardize things. With a standard presentation, we could better evaluate how everyone was doing, and we'd also have a much more effective way to alter the presentation across the company if we needed to.

When I announced that we were going to move to a single, company-wide presentation, it almost caused a mutiny. Forget taking over public relations. Some guys took this as an act of war. And to be honest, I understood where they were coming from. There were plenty of SGAs who were having success doing it their way and had been for years. Now I'm asking them to do something new. This flew in the face of the old adage, "If it ain't broke, don't fix it."

The trouble was, the presentation wasn't broken from an individual territory perspective, but it was broken from a company perspective. And since I ran the company, it was up to me to fix it. It was such a contentious subject, so I started out trying to be as transparent as possible when creating the new presentation. We met with SGAs for months and months, looking at their presentations to piece together the best parts of each one, but that became a mess. Every guy thought theirs was best and they wanted more of what worked for them in the final product. Then there were guys who hated the whole idea of what I was trying to do, so they sabotaged the discussions at every turn. Eventually, I had to cut off that line of communication and tell them that no matter how much stalling or delaying or second-guessing they did, we were going to have one, uniform presentation and they were going to have to use it.

As a leader, I really had to steel myself with this whole process. It was one of those situations where I knew in my bones that I was right, and I just had to ignore all the doubters. I believed in my vision more than anybody else, and I was prepared to do whatever I could to execute it.

The two big wins I wanted to get out of a uniform presentation was a decrease in complaints about agent misinformation, and an increase in referrals, since they'd be built into the presentation across the whole company.

The process to install the new presentation took about a year. Once it was being run everywhere, we saw a huge increase in referrals, which was certainly a form of validation for me. In the beginning, we didn't see much of a bump when it came to closing, but I knew that was because a lot of the older agents weren't as confident doing it this way. In this scenario, our agent churn actually helped my cause. We turned over about 90% of our agency force year over year. That meant that by the second year of using the new presentation, 90% of the workforce was trained with it and didn't know anything about the old system. In the end, the benefits we got from having one presentation far outweighed any reason to stick with the old system. Realistically, however, the reason all of this was possible was because of technology; specifically, laptop computers, which had come down in price to the point where all of our agents could own one and run their presentation from it. This was monumental for us.

Prior to basic laptops becoming affordable, agents would go into the field with huge binders that they'd use as a reference point for their presentation. Inside the binder was all of the brochures and freebies that agents would give away as they went through the presentation. The system worked fine, but it clearly wasn't as efficient as having the whole thing on a laptop and presented on a screen for the clients.

I brought in a guy to head up the whole transition to laptops, and he eventually became the vice president of another company that I took over. As always, there was pushback everywhere, but we knew the future of our presentations was digital, so I just said, "I'm gonna do this, guys. You can either have input or not."

Some gave input and some didn't, but we put together a blueprint of how the whole thing would look on a laptop and then assembled it. We also got rid of the thousands of paper applications we received each week, which dramatically streamlined our entire administrative process. The critical part was that we could now ask for referrals right there in the presentation. Sometimes agents felt weird about this part, but having a referral prompt pop up on the screen helped. Now, they just had to click on it and type in the names the policyholder gave them. This was fairly easy and got them into the habit of asking for referrals.

As we became more focused on referrals, another component to our master equation came into focus: The more agents we had, the more referrals we could get, and the more policies we could sell. That meant that we needed to supercharge our hiring process in order to see exponential growth as a company.

For that, we brought in a guy named Bo Gentile. I hired him from a company called Manpower and he became our dedicated recruiter. His only thought was taking the agency force from 1,100 agents to 7,500 agents.

We knew that having more agents would grow the company, and we looked at hiring month over month: How many new agents did we hire, terminate, and how many do we have left?

We wanted to grow the agency force 10% to 20% per year. Bo's plan to do this was for us to essentially become a recruiting company that sells insurance. Everything we did was geared toward being able to increase the agent count. It was simple:

If we can increase the agent count, we will grow this company. If we can't, we won't.

All of our recruiting was now data driven. We set up a system where we were downloading hundreds of thousands of resumes from Monster and distributing them to the SGAs. We were one of Monster's biggest clients because we really needed to get people into the field with the SGAs. We needed to train them to recruit on a mass scale. The entire operation was a big success.

Between the standard presentation on the laptops, the referrals, the centralized public relations, the massive increase in hiring, and the revamped SGA and MGA system, I was really proud of the direction we'd pulled the company in my first three to five years. We were experiencing 10% growth or more every year, and we knocked on the $100 million mark a few times before breaking it. One year we were $97 million. Another year we were $96.

After the second or third year where we fell short of the $100 million, I announced the new goal to be $250 million and then we blew passed it. This was a valuable lesson for business and life. The moment you get close to your goal, you have to immediately increase it or you won't go anywhere.

One of the earliest moves I made while all these changes were taking place was to create an Executive Council. The Executive Council changed every year. It could be top SGAs from the bigger territories, or lower territories, but you had to have growth to get on this council. I would take my ideas to this council, and there were some real knockdown, drag out fights about whether my ideas were good or if their ideas were better.

These SGAs were the kings of their own kingdoms. If I could get buy-in from them collectively, we could make things happen because the other SGAs looked up them. If the Executive Council's SGAs were on board, the company got moving. I was constantly talking to them, but twice a year I'd have full Executive Council meetings because I knew that if you didn't get buy-in, you'd get backstabbing.

During these meetings I always had a plan for where I wanted to be at the end, but it was rare that I'd walk out in line with my original idea. At the end, their solutions were a lot better. They were the boots on the ground.

A lot of times, when the meetings were over, the end result was a mix of all of our ideas. This was new for me. It took me a while to go from pretending to want to hear everyone's ideas to really, truly wanting to hear them. My instinct was to present my idea and drag everyone along until they agreed. Looking back, that is horrible leadership! I can say now that one of the toughest things I had to learn was to keep an open mind and not ram my ideas down others' throats. Once I learned to do that, the meetings became profoundly productive and some of our best ideas as a company came out of them.

I believe that one of the reasons I was able to get the best from the Executive Council as the years wore on was the trust factor.

Trust isn't just about keeping your word.

Trust is about your team believing that the vision you presented was going to be better for them *and* better for the company. The only way this works is by having success. Obviously, you're not going to hit a home run every time, but you have to hit the ball more times than you miss, and that's what I did.

Because we had more successes than defeats, the SGAs were able to grow their agencies with these systems and ideas. When I'd bring up the next big idea, they'd be more amenable to it because we now had a track record of success. I could also point to how the past changes had benefited them.

Let me show you how your renewals have grown.

Let me show you how your advances have grown.

Let me show you how many agents we've promoted.

As long as your ideas work a majority of the time, you have trust. If you have trust, you have influence. And if you have the organizational teams behind your ideas, then you have a really good chance of growing the company.

Most importantly, you need someone you trust to organize your time. As a leader, your number one most valuable asset is your time, and if you don't invest in somebody who can efficiently help you manage your hours and days, you're dead in the water.

In those first few years, my life was a whirlwind of meetings and traveling, and I would not have been able to accomplish a fraction of what I needed to without Ginny Castillo, my executive assistant. Ginny could talk to any person with grace and aplomb. She could talk to a single agent in the company who had a problem, or someone like Nancy Pelosi's Chief of Staff. She could handle it all.

There were times when I'd be on the road so long that I'd truly forget what city I was in and where I was going next. On any given day there could be forty, fifty, or sixty people trying to get ahold of me—from SGAs to people in the labor movement or politics. To have someone like Ginny who could organize my life was invaluable. It allowed me the thinking time I needed to dwell on my decisions and be free to do the job.

Without Ginny, I would not have been able to do anything. I'd have been a frazzled mess trying to organize my travel and my schedule and my meetings…and my life, really. I didn't want to end this section without giving her the credit she deserves for helping me throughout this journey.

CHAPTER 16

Mantras, Leadership & Conventions

While I was reshaping the future of American Income, I was also trying to create a fun childhood for my kids. I figured I owed it to them after all the moves, so my gift to them was the Spitting Llama Ranch. I bought the fifty-acre ranch when we moved to Waco, and it was a really special place for us. It was on the Brazos River, and we had goats and horses and, of course, llamas. We had plenty of room to go four-wheeling and one time even set up a paintball course.

The house itself was a big, two-story place that featured blue tiles from the Caribbean that I thought looked great. Adam and Emily had a lot of room to roam, and Emily had a secret room right off her bedroom. We had the ranch for three or four years, and I have very fond memories of living there. At that time, I was spending about one week in New York City each month, and it always struck me as interesting how I could go from being in the busiest city in the world, and then four hours later I was driving to our ranch out in the country, passing every species of cow known to man!

As I started making the changes to American Income and eventually moved up to become President and CEO, I was getting a lot of pressure to move to McKinney, where the executive offices were. Eventually I caved, and we moved into an old stone house on a couple acres of land. It was a nice house, but nothing memorable. It had high ceilings with a giant stone design along the front.

It was during the years in Waco and McKinney that I really found my footing as the leader of American Income (and soon another company, which I'll get to). Experience, of course, always helps. But I also realized that, as a leader, I was going to have to concentrate on two big things if I wanted to take the company to new heights. I was going to have to build trust with the workforce, and I was going to have to provide the company with a new vision every year.

I'll start with building trust.

On Trust

I've written about trust in this book from several vantage points, including how we fostered trust with the unions, and how devastated I was when I felt I could no longer trust Mr. Rapoport's word. All of these lessons stayed with me when I became an executive, and aside from my initiatives to improve the company, one of my first orders of business was to establish trust with our agents and agencies. In order to do this, I essentially turned the company into a large agency and ran it like a super territory.

Early on, I flew every SGA to the home office for one-on-one meetings. They'd usually arrive in the afternoon, and then I'd take them out to dinner at Three Forks, a great steak restaurant. This was really a let's-just-talk type of dinner. I asked a lot of questions and did a lot of listening. That wasn't the time for me to be the heavy-handed boss. I'd ask them about their families and their goals and where they wanted to go with the company. I'd even ask about what pissed them off and let them vent a little.

When dinner was over we'd usually have a cigar, and I'd share my vision for the company. I tried to keep things casual to put the SGAs at ease. It certainly helped that I eventually became friends with the guy who owned Three Forks, so it began to feel like an extension of my living room. Even though the evening was relaxing, I was paying very close attention to how the SGAs answered a lot of my questions and how they responded to my comments about the future of the company.

As I explained my vision, I made it a point to be open and honest about what I expected from them. This was a fine line I had to walk because, for most of these SGAs, just the idea that I was sitting with them for a one-on-one was totally new. In fact, the relationship that I was proposing was going to be brand new for them as well. I knew that it was going to be a little jarring at first and that there would be an adjustment period for most of these SGAs. That being said, it was important for me to explain what my goals for the company were and to convince them to buy in.

"This is the direction I'm going and I'd like to have you with me," I'd say. "But if after hearing everything I'm saying you don't feel that you can get on board, then you need to get off the bus."

Unfortunately, there were a lot of SGAs who would agree with me to my face, but I could tell that deep down they were still going to do things their way. That wasn't going to work. I wanted to take the company to the next level, and I had no time for anchors. In the end, I terminated about half of the SGA body that first year, and we didn't miss a beat. Actually, we continued to grow. Getting rid of some of the dead weight and bad attitudes allowed new blood to come in. This was refreshing for me and the individual agencies.

After that first year, I decided to take my show on the road and started the "Roger Smith Run Your Ass Ragged Tour," on which I made it my goal to sit down face-to-face with every SGA in their home office.

I realize that this may sound overwhelming, but I really enjoyed it. Traveling, being with the agents, leading meetings and observing meetings —this was my environment. It's crazy to write this, but I always felt more comfortable on the road and on the move than being in one place.

On those trips, I'd fly into a territory in the afternoon and take the SGA out for a one-on-one steak dinner in the evening. That dinner was similar to the one I had with the SGAs at Three Forks—similar conversation, similar goals. The next day I would speak at their agency, meeting with all of the agents and the management team. If I had time, I'd take just the managers out to dinner, but if not, I'd fly out. That was the system I developed, and it was very effective.

It allowed me to get a good feel for the agency in a short period of time and assess any red flags that I noticed. When you're in a leadership position, you get very good at sensing when something isn't right among the troops. For me, there were a few solid "tells."

The number one most obvious tell was when an SGA was either negative about the new ideas I was presenting, or if they were passive-aggressive about them. I understood that some people had a negative perception of the home office, and I certainly didn't expect them to look at me like a knight in shining armor, but quite often a person's body language betrays how they really feel.

If they have their arms crossed the whole time I'm talking, or if they're leaning back in their chair or their eyes are darting around, those are red flags that tell me I'm not getting through to them. Or, that I've gotten through to them and they just don't like what I'm saying.

People who are genuinely interested and excited about listening to you tend to lean in close. They smile a lot. They ask a lot of questions. They have good energy. There was a big difference between negative and positive people.

Next to face time with the SGA, the best place to evaluate an agency was at the agency itself. It was rare that I'd come away unimpressed from our dinner and then be overwhelmed at how well the agency was run.

When I went to an SGA's Monday meeting, I could sense immediately if it was a positive or negative environment. It was in the air. Were agents happy to be there? Was the tone of the meeting motivational or stifling? Was anybody laughing and having a good time? Was there any camaraderie between the agents? If the answer to most of these questions was yes, there was a decent chance the SGA would get on board.

If the answer to most or all of these questions was no, then I knew that this person wasn't going to survive under my leadership. But it wasn't as if I had dinner with an SGA and simply said, "you're gone" after seeing their meeting the next day. I sat down with them and set goals. I typically gave them a ninety-day plan or a six-month plan for where they needed to be. If they didn't make it, all that did was confirm my suspicions.

If they jumped in and made immediate changes, I knew they'd see improvement because we'd tested the new strategies in other territories and with other agencies. A lot of guys claimed they implemented the new strategies, but their numbers were flat or even went down, and I knew they hadn't really embraced anything. Rather, they were checking off the boxes without getting their agents excited.

Within a few years, after the company turnover and the culling of SGAs, I finally had a workforce that was as close to 100% on board with my vision as we were going to get.

And it showed in our growth, which is something I'm very proud of. It meant that I was able to get our whole company to buy into the vision I had. I did this with yearly mantras.

THE MOST UNLIKELY LEADER

On Mantras

I loved mantras, and I loved coming up with mantras. What better way to get the whole company pulling in the same direction than to come up with a mantra or slogan that everyone can rally around. To me, mantras were efficient and effective. They gave me a chance to distill an entire goal or strategy or theme for the year into a few memorable, catchy words or even a phrase.

I also loved mantras because they motived people at every level of the company. If you picked the right slogan, it could motivate an SGA and a new hire with exactly the same energy. We'd have one mantra for all of American Income. It would be written on a white board in the home office, at an agency in San Francisco, at an agency in San Antonio—everywhere. The same mantra would be used in the biggest offices in Boston and at a smaller satellite office in Boise. It united us. Wherever you went, the whole company was on the same page.

One of my favorite mantras that I came up with early in my tenure was, "Step Up So Others Can Step In." At the time, we had a lot of agents who never moved up because, as I wrote about earlier, the incentives were out of whack. I believed that having too many people in positions where they felt like they had no shot at a promotion would cause stasis in the organization.

That's why I came up with "Step Up So Others Can Step In." The mantra was aimed at pretty much everybody. We had agencies where an SGA had one MGA and one GA, and that was it. He stopped there, and maybe everyone was happy and maybe they weren't, but if you were a new hire and you wanted to move up in that agency, you were kind of screwed. My goal with that mantra was to get everyone thinking bigger.

I wanted SGAs to think, *I need to grow so that I can hire more MGAs and GAs*. I wanted MGAs to think, *I want to get promoted to SGA so I can promote one of my agents to MGA*.

That kind of thinking had a snowball effect on the company. It was inspiring and made everyone feel like we were in this together. If you stepped up your game, you'd be rewarded and so would the people around you.

Another one of my favorites was "Opportunity Unlimited." This was actually a phrase that Mr. Rapoport came up with, and it meant that if you've got the work ethic and you're willing to put in the time to learn our systems, and you're coachable, the sky is the limit. I cut my teeth on that phrase, and I loved it because it reinforced what I always believed. It was personal to me because it really embodied my career with American Income. The opportunity provided by the company can take you as far as you're willing to go. In essence, you had your destiny in your own hands with us.

"Think Big" was a mantra I stole from one of our SGAs, Rick Altig. He was one of my most successful SGAs and the most creative. We sometimes had an adversarial relationship, but he was a big-time producer and I valued his thoughts.

Conventions

In addition to the mantras, the biggest and flashiest motivational tool we had was our yearly convention. My thinking was that my agents have worked hard all year, and getting to attend a convention was the top reward. If you earned an invite to a convention, it was special. The location was going to be exciting and nice and feel like a big destination event. That was the main reason I loved having them: My agents deserved them!

The second reason I loved our convention was that it allowed us to hand out awards. If you've worked your ass off all year and you get to go onstage in front of a couple thousand of your peers to accept an award, that's a big moment. I think a lot of corporations that don't have a convention don't truly understand the value. When you think about it, what really motivates people?

Money, for sure.

We're all motivated by money, especially in a sales position. But recognition is an equally big motivator. To ensure that the awards didn't just go to agencies in the biggest markets, we broke things down into categories based on population. That meant we'd have the top five SGAs, top five MGAs, and top five RGAs from all different market sizes getting awards. This gave every territory equal representation. Winners would take home a plaque or a crystal vase, and we made sure they were really classy looking.

And the third reason I loved the convention goes along with my idea about mantras. When you have a convention, you get several thousand of your top agents together and you have a captive audience for two or three days. You can't beat that when it comes to getting your message out to the whole company. Truth be told, the conventions were set up specifically to maximize every aspect of the things I mentioned above.

The first night of the convention was our reception. This was usually the day when everyone flew in, and we dedicated that night for people to mingle and catch up. It was free-flowing and allowed people to really see the scope and size of American Income. It was exciting on several levels. We had longtime agents who only saw each other once a year, and first-time attendees mixing with executives.

When an agent qualified for a convention, the company also paid for their spouse to attend, so there was that added aspect. As I touched upon earlier in the book, being an agent isn't easy, especially in the beginning when you're out giving presentations five nights a week. You miss a lot of family time. By flying an agent's husband or wife in, they got to be rewarded as well for holding down the fort . I always enjoyed watching the spouses meet and share experiences. That's when some real friendships were formed.

The second night of the convention was the general meeting, where there were typically three or four speeches planned by company executives. We'd have the head of public relations speak, and then the vice president, and then I'd give my remarks and introduce the keynote speaker. I loved this part of the night because we were usually able to secure a terrific speaker for the company.

One year we got my hero Zig Ziglar to speak. Another year we got John C. Maxwell. We even got Mike Eruzione from the 1980 US Olympic Hockey Team to give a big motivational talk.

Some years we opted to skip the speaker and we'd put on some kind of performance or skit that required audience involvement. One year I did a *Tonight Show* bit, and I had a desk like Johnny Carson and a couch where we had the top agents up as guests. I kept the flow moving, and it was really successful.

Another time we held the convention in New York City, and we brought everyone to Broadway and took over a theater for the night. The following convention, we went to Vegas and hired the best impersonators to go onstage and do a routine. One year the entertainment was a group that performed songs from famous Broadway plays. They ended with *Phantom of the Opera,* and we set up a little bit of our own showmanship. At the end of the performance, the room went almost dark, and while people were distracted I switched places with the actor who played the phantom. When the lights came back on, I took off my mask and revealed that I was the phantom the whole time. The audience loved it!

The entertainment and the speakers always went over big. The whole goal was to be energetic and have fun and reward everybody for a job well done.

And these things weren't cheap!

A convention could cost anywhere from $3 million to $5 million. There was a travel person at Torchmark whose job it was to secure locations for the conventions. They'd do a bunch of research on their own, and then they'd give me five options and I'd pick the most glamorous locations. My number one goal was for it to be magnificent and motivating. Some cities are fun, but not for a convention like this. For instance, Nashville is a cool city, but would you rather go to Nashville or Cancún?

During my time at the helm, the cost of the conventions was brought up several times. Accountants and executive penny pinchers thought canceling them was an easy way to lower our expenses, but I refused.

"Is it really necessary?" they'd ask.

"Yes," was my answer each and every time.

Every other year I'd run a six-month contest to get a lot of production during the last quarter of a given year and the first quarter of the next year.. I limited this contest to just thirty people (sixty with spouses), and we'd take an extravagant trip to Spain or France or go on a cruise. I never wanted those to feel like part of the routine, so I only did them sporadically.

While the conventions and contests were about rewarding our agents, I also wanted to make sure that as a company we were giving back. Corporate donations were nothing new, but one year when Mark McAndrew and I were leaving a convention, I had an experience that changed things for me.

The convention was at a beautiful, luxurious resort in the tropics, and as we drove to the airport the poverty around us was heartbreaking. It really hit me. Here we were, hosting thousands of people in a first-class way—eating steaks, drinking expensive tequila, having a great time in a foreign country—and the people who lived there had nothing. It left a bad taste in my mouth.

From that point on, wherever we had a meeting, we did our research and found a local charity we could help raise money for. I'd put out the call to the SGAs, the executive council, and the individual agents: "I'm not going to tell you how much to contribute. I don't care if it's $5 or $5,000, but as a company we're going to support this group and leave that city better than when we showed up."

I was brought to tears every year by the amount of money we raised. Then Torchmark began contributing to the total amount and the donation numbers skyrocketed. When I'd present the check to these groups, many of them would tell me that it was like a gift from heaven.

We donated to homeless shelters, military veteran groups, and one year contributed to an organization that trained seeing-eye dogs. We fully funded one dog, and they named him Bernard, after Mr. Rapoport. That one was really special. I've even stayed in touch with several of the organizations in my retirement.

CHAPTER 17

Taking Over Liberty

If you've taken away one theme from this book so far, it's likely that I was always on the move. Whether personally or professionally, I was constantly in expansion mode. I think it's just how I'm wired. As soon as I began to reach my goals and be successful at something, I began to look for more opportunities.

During my tenure at the top of American Income, I began paying attention to one of the sister companies that Torchmark owned, Liberty National Life Insurance. Liberty is one of the oldest insurance companies in America, with roots that go all the way back to 1900 when it was founded in Birmingham, Alabama.

Liberty was also the oldest of the five companies owned by Torchmark. It was a completely different vibe and setup than American Income. It was the kind of place where there were three generations of people at the company. It had the feel of an old southern debit company where the pace was slow and the people sort of plodded along. There was more of a "beat the system" attitude.

The other major difference was that all of the agents were salaried employees, and every single one of them had a nine-to-five mentality. They punched in and they punched out. They didn't work nights. They didn't work weekends. It was a completely ineffective way to run a sales organization.

Over the years, the leadership at Torchmark had gone to great lengths to try to fix it. Nothing worked, and there was a ton of infighting. Before I arrived, the president of the company and the chief actuarial wouldn't talk to each other. So, the one person in charge of risk and money was making decisions while the other person who was in charge of marketing that workforce was doing his own thing, often to the detriment of the company's profitability.

The place was hemorrhaging money. For every dollar of premiums they sold, it was costing them $1.13. And yet all of the agents were on salary and went about their business. If they made a few sales in a day, great. If they didn't, no big deal, they were getting paid anyway. Liberty was so unprofitable that Torchmark considered selling it several times.

Meanwhile, I was having a great run at American Income, but I was keeping an eye on Liberty. Something inside was telling me that I could turn them around if given the chance. When the chatter grew louder that Torchmark was going to sell it, I threw my hat in the ring to run the company.

My thought was, *I know I can run American Income, let me see if I can make something out of Liberty.*

It was going to be one of my biggest achievements. I loved the challenge. For Torchmark, it was a final chance to see if someone could turn their oldest company around. The biggest concern leadership at Torchmark had was whether I could run both AIL *and* Liberty. By that time, we'd turned American Income into the most profitable company under the Torchmark banner. We were growing 10% to 20% every year. I understood their concern, but I knew I could do it, and every time they tried to talk me out of it, I said, "I got this." Eventually I wore them down and they let me give it a shot.

What I wanted to do with Liberty was nothing short of a complete and total reimaging of the culture and workforce. As it stood, there were agents who had been hanging on for three decades, making a sale a week with no pressure to produce any more, getting a salary, raking in huge bonuses, and punching out at 5 p.m. every day. Every hour they were on the clock they were losing the company money—and they'd been doing it for thirty years! It still seems unfathomable, but that's the way it was.

The first thing I had to do was explain that the old system was going away, but that it was going to be replaced with a system that offered them more opportunity. And by more opportunity, I meant the chance to earn more money. I knew the only way I was going to convince agents to come on board was to put it to them this way: "Listen, I know you made X amount every year guaranteed. Now, with this new commission structure, you can make two times X if you put in the work."

This was a complete 180 from the way these agents had been doing things. Truth be told, the only way the commission structure worked was if each agent was selling enough policies to make it profitable. As I got my hands deeper into Liberty, I could see that the employee mindset was going to be a hard thing to break for a lot of people. They were so used to collecting a check with minimum output that many of them weren't going to be able to adjust to the new model. The mentality of going from a guaranteed paycheck, regardless of their sales numbers, to increased production requirements and less of a guarantee was scary for a lot of them.

One thing I did have in my favor was that a lot of the Liberty branch managers had been watching their American Income SGA counterparts earn well into six-figures a year. I was lucky that a core group of employees at Liberty said, "I want that," and became very enthusiastic about what I was doing.

To help shift the culture away from "employee-based" to "entrepreneur-minded," we made some changes to the language we used. The Liberty Equivalent of an SGA had the title of branch manager, which was about as uninspiring as it gets! We swapped that out for "Agency Owner," and the shift really worked. I know it's semantics, but when a person can call themselves an "owner" of something they inherently take more responsibility for its success. This type of buy-in is much more powerful than "managing" something. When you're a manager, you are typically managing for someone else. You're managing their money or their product or their workforce. It was important for me that the Liberty agents understood that they were in control of their agencies and their futures.

After that shift, we began using commission-based language, and we implemented all the tools from American Income that worked and produced results. By the end of the first year, we'd moved 90% of the branch managers over to the "agency owner" title, and we were training new agents on the new system.

Pretty soon, just as I'd anticipated, the new guys who had never heard of the old system were quickly outselling and outworking the old guys who wouldn't let go of the salary structure. Some of the old-timers were milking the clock, trying to hang on to their paycheck and ballooned bonus payments for as long as they could. They'd been gaming the system for so long, and they didn't know any other way. I knew what was going on, and I finally said, "We're changing the bonus structure. We're rewarding hard work from now on. You're either on the bus or off."

I also used the model of the leadership school we'd been running at American Income and brought it to Liberty. Within two years, you couldn't tell the difference between an AIL leadership school and a Liberty leadership school. It was terrific to watch the transformation.

I had half a building for American Income, and I put Liberty's offices in the other half right down the hall. Because I was running both companies, I had to walk a fine line with Liberty and assure them that I wasn't turning them into American Income. After all, they had a brand and a storied history that they were proud of, as they should have been. They wanted to protect their legacy, and I understood that. I told them that my job was to help them install winning systems in their company, not to change the brand.

As I shook things up, our retention rate of new hires stayed in the 10% to 14% range, which was the same as American Income. I did have quite a bit of turnover in the agency/owner body and the level beneath that, but that was expected. These were the old-guard types who'd been scamming the system for years. Before me, Liberty had three or four different presidents in about five years, so these old guys were looking at me as if I was just another guy who would come in, talk a lot, and be gone in a year or so. Once they realized that I meant business and that the systems I was implementing worked, they knew they were in trouble.

The fact that I was from American Income and had an entire company as proof of my methods made them realize that the changes were inevitable and permanent. That's why it was really, really important in the beginning to take at least four or five guys, make them agency owners, and coach them up to have success. If that handful of guys can implement our recruiting systems, sales systems, and everything else to build their agencies, then we'd have credibility within Liberty and be off and running. Fortunately, these guys didn't have the back-end charges and other hindrances I had to weed out at American Income. They had a totally different deal. Six months down the line they'd be getting their renewals, which helped us show that we knew what we were doing.

The greatest joy I had at Liberty came from the guys who stuck with me from my first day and the early hires I made who bought into the vision and believed in it with me. I was fortunate in that I was able to convince Steve DeChiaro to leave his spot as the SGA in Denver to become my right-hand man at Liberty. I also pulled Mike Sheets, who was in charge of putting American Income onto the laptop presentation, over to Liberty to help Steve. I had the executive team we needed to succeed. Dolores Skarjune was a critical operations leader with me as well.

Five years after we took over, the company was completely transformed and profitable. There were people who were on a sub-six figure salary when we got there now making a million dollars a year.

That was endlessly gratifying to see, and it hammered home one of the main philosophies of my career as a leader: Do what you say you're going to do! We said that if they trusted us, we'd take them to the Promised Land, and we did.

As a leader, there is no better feeling in the world.

With Liberty and American Income firing on all cylinders, I was feeling grateful and gratified with everything we'd been able to accomplish. By this time, we were knocking on that $250 million goal that I'd set all those years back when we finally crossed the $100 million line, and I'd begun to think about my future, as well as the company's future. Despite our success, I knew deep down that for American Income to blast past $250 million and eventually $500 million and beyond, it was going to take someone younger than me and someone who could better navigate the new corporate culture that was taking over so many companies in America.

When we took over the company, Mark McAndrew and I would sit down at the end of every year and decide who was getting promoted, what their bonuses were, and what their salary increases were. Toward the end of my tenure, things had changed dramatically. I recall a specific instance when I wanted to promote a woman to a Vice President role, and rather than being able to simply call her and tell her the good news, the new rules said that all Vice President promotions had to be approved by a committee, which comprised people from human resources, accounting, sales, etc.

I'm not judging one way or the other the merits of this

system—it clearly works for a lot of people and a lot of corporations. It just didn't work for me and how I'd become accustomed to doing things during my career. As more of these kinds of instances came up, I realized it was probably time for me to move on.

Fortunately, Larry Hutchison and Gary Coleman, the co-CEOs of Torchmark, were great guys and were willing to work with me. They gave me a two-year consulting deal to allow me to ease my way out while the new blood, Steve Greer and David Zophin, moved in. I am extremely grateful to them for allowing me to do that.

It gave me time to figure out what I was going to do, and it made me feel good to know the right guys were taking my place. I knew that the next generation understood our legacy and was going to build on it. As the leader of a company, that's all you can ask for on your way out.

CHAPTER 18

Blessed

When I look back on my career, there are things I got to do on a regular basis that I took for granted. For years I ate at the best restaurants in every city I went. I stayed at the finest hotels. I traveled first class. I traveled around the world. My schedule was grueling at times, but as I drove down memory lane for this book, I realized that I can't complain about living the high life—especially since I spent so much of my early life too drugged out to appreciate anything.

Even though I wasn't a sports fan, a lot of my SGAs were, and I attended too many football and baseball games to count. I must have been to a half-dozen Steelers games over the years because our SGA in Pittsburgh was a diehard fan.

My connections with the labor movement also allowed for some fantastic experiences. I went to the Democratic National Convention every election, and I've had working relationships with many of the important politicians of our time. I mentioned my work with Bill Clinton back in Arkansas, but more recently I was able to have Speaker of the House Nancy Pelosi and Senator Harry Reid talk at my meetings. That was a real thrill, as I've been interested in social change and liberal politics since I was a teenager. That was something that my mother and Andy instilled in me early on.

One of the absolute highlights of my life was being able to attend an exclusive fundraiser with Barack Obama. There I was, a kid from nowhere who was an ex-addict and juvenile delinquent, who didn't graduate high school or college, and I was at a high-end event with only fifteen other people sitting at a table with the future president of the United States.

Talk about a natural high!

Another time through my connections, I found myself in a meeting with a half-dozen other people, and one of them was Hillary Clinton. That was a real honor. Those were the days when I was really connected to some high-powered people and that I felt like I was helping to do good in the world.

Looking back, I got to spend time and have quality conversations with some important leaders in the labor movement. These were some of the greatest labor leaders of our time. John Sweeney was the president of the national AFL-CIO. Rich Trumka, who was president of the mine workers union and later became president of the AFL-CIO, was someone I was privileged to know. To be able to spend time with these prominent members of our labor advisory board, who spent their lives fighting the injustices of this world, was beyond inspiring. I had a lot of admiration for how they spent their lives in the trenches.

One trip I'll never forget was going to Israel with Jimmy Hoffa's family. These kinds of experiences were so personal to me. I can't overstate the importance they hold in my heart.

When it came time to retire, I knew that I was not only retiring from my position as leader of two massive companies but from my lifestyle as well. No more spending thirty or forty weeks on the road. No more company meetings and mantras. No more of everything I'd known for the past few decades, really.

This brought up a bit of an identity crisis.

If I wasn't running a company, who was I?

I was a father, first and foremost. Admittedly, and as you've no doubt surmised, I often prioritized my career and traveling over staying home with my different wives and kids. When I reflect on all the times I was away when

I could have been home, I have a sense of unmistakable remorse. I love all my children, but I have always felt more comfortable on the road and on the move.

I have been a husband five times, and it's only with this fifth marriage that I've realized how much you have to work to make them successful. It's an odd thing to put your life down on paper. Even though I'm the one living my life, I never stopped to examine it like this before, and one thing I've noticed is that throughout all the turmoil and traveling and jobs, I was never alone.

I went from one wife to a girlfriend who became a wife to another girlfriend. I went from one state to another state to another job. I've repeated this pattern my whole life, and it's only now, looking back, that I can appreciate how my actions and motivations have affected everyone around me. My wives. My kids. My co-workers. Everyone.

I'm proud of what I've accomplished, but it came at a cost, for sure. I think that's the tradeoff with any endeavor. I do believe that every year I tried to get better, both personally and professionally. When I got married a fifth time, I was determined to do it right, all the way down to legally adopting my wife's daughter Amiah.

This was important to me because Andy Smith never legally adopted me. I have his last name, but nothing on paper that says I'm his son. That has gnawed at me my whole life. Why didn't he adopt me? It's just one of those things that hurts and makes you question your worth. When I married De, I already knew that I wanted to adopt Amiah because I never wanted her to feel about me the way I did about Andy.

These are the things we think about as we get older. We want to right the wrongs. We want to learn from mistakes we've made and mistakes we've been the victim of.

One of the biggest transitions for me in retirement has been my focus on God and religion, which I never gave much thought to for most of my life. I see now that even when I didn't believe, God was watching over me and helping me. That has been a transformative experience, and I'm blessed to have Him in my life. One quick anecdote about this shift: For years and years, I worked closely with an SGA named Jim Surace, who became an ordained minister. When he would show up to a meeting I would actually avoid him! I knew he'd want to talk about God and Jesus, and I wasn't ready for it at that time in my life.

Later on, it was his influence and De's influence that really opened up my eyes and my heart to God.

The final piece of the puzzle comes in the form of a question I suppose we all have to ask when we end a chapter in our lives:

What do I do now?

For me, I began to tackle my bucket list items one-by-one.

I've become more involved in charities that are near and dear to me, including a mentorship program for young men that I'm very proud of.

For years, I've dreamt of becoming an actor but never had the time. In my retirement, I've begun taking acting lessons at the Burt Reynolds Jupiter Theatre. It has been wonderful to get back onstage and challenge myself to learn a new craft. I even got a part in a local performance of Glengarry Glen Ross, and I enjoyed the hell out of it.

I've always toyed with the idea of opening a cigar bar, and I've gone so far as to talk to the owner of the local shop I frequent about his business. I don't know if that will lead to anything, but it's one of those threads I may keep pulling at if time permits.

And at the top of my bucket list was writing this book!

The fact that you're holding it in your hands gives me tremendous pride. I've wanted to tell my story for as long as I can remember. Being able to share my trials and tribulations with you has been an honor.

Thank you for reading.

This book has been predominantly about business and my life and my career, and I made a conscious decision to leave my children out of most of it. I mentioned a few of our homes and milestones along the way, but I felt it best to focus on me and my trials and tribulations. I love each of my children dearly, and I am blessed to have them in my life. One day, if they so choose, they can tell their own stories from their perspectives. But that will be their choice.

That being said, I wanted to share a brief story about each child for posterity, because these illustrate something I love about them.

Adam

This story is a great example of how I knew Adam was going to be a principled man when he grew up. It takes place when Adam was getting ready to buy his first car. I told him that I would spend between $6,000 and $12,000 on a car for him. At the same time, his mother was bugging him about going on a mission trip with a local church. Adam didn't want to go and had several reasons why it made him uncomfortable.

After telling her no, his mom got in my ear and started pushing me to help convince him to go on the trip. So, I explained to Adam that I could either buy him the cheap car, or he could make my life a little easier by going on the mission trip, and I would buy him the more expensive car.

His instantaneous response was that he guessed he would be driving the cheap car!

At first, I felt embarrassed that I had tried to buy off my son (for a good cause, at least) but then was immensely proud that he stuck to his guns and wouldn't let me get away with it. That was the day I knew what kind of man he would become, and he hasn't disappointed me since.

Conrad

I remember asking Conrad when he was about ten years old what he wanted to be when he grew up. He responded that he would like to be either a CEO like me or a forest ranger. One would take care of his desire to have wealth, and the other would fulfill a passion he has for the outdoors. It made me realize how blessed I was to have a career that could fulfill both things for me.

Conrad is still working to find something that satisfies both desires (as most people are), but he's married to a wonderful woman and figured out one thing long before I did: love.

Emily

Emily's story actually sounds like a punchline to a joke. For many years she wanted to be a child psychologist and was progressing in that direction. After my divorce with her mother, she changed her focus to masculine studies and did her dissertation and doctorate on that subject.

I think she is still trying to figure me out!

The one thing that struck me was her ability to persevere. While she was getting her doctorate, the person who was supposed to be guiding her through the process of her dissertation ended up becoming the biggest hindrance to her success. He had his own selfish motives and was trying to sabotage her.

It was a tough spot.

What do you do when the person who holds the keys to your kingdom refuses to hand them over?

In her case, she fought through. She was the perfect example of keeping your eyes on the prize and having the determination to get there.

The reward is we now call her Dr. Smith.

Nicole

Nicole's is the story that hits closest to home, as she has fought through years of addiction and, as of this writing, will soon be celebrating one year of sobriety. She is such a great person to be around, and yet there were many times in the past twenty years that I just wanted to give up.

I'm blessed that God showed me mercy. I get angry with myself for being so calloused as to want to give up on her when God himself hadn't. I know her life won't be easy, but at least we will go through the ups and downs together from now on.

Amiah

This is the most recent story, and it unfolded as I listened to my daughter Amiah negotiate a deal with her mom, De. And let me tell you, De is not the easiest person to negotiate with!

It had to do with a boy, and I was so impressed with her poise and demeanor. She talked like a mature adult, didn't get emotional about what she wanted, kept levity in her voice, and provided other options in the negotiation.

In the end, she didn't get what she wanted, but she handled it better than most adults would have.

As I write this, she will be heading off to college in a few months. She's not sure yet about her career, but after listening to that conversation I feel secure that she will be able to negotiate her way through life no matter what obstacles are put in her way.

ACKNOWLEDGEMENTS

I have so many people to thank for my successes in life, and since this is my book, I'm going to take the time to do it.

First, I'd like to dedicate this book to all the people who have influenced me, and to all the people I have been blessed to influence. Believe me, I don't take any of it for granted.

Thank you to my mentors (Mike Ferrone, Bernard Rapoport, and Mark McAndrew).

A special thanks to Steve Greer and David Zophin at American Income, and Steve DiChiaro and Mike Sheets at Liberty National. There is no better gift than to watch you take what we built together and improve on it in remarkable ways.

A special thank you to the SGAs of American Income and the Agency Owners of Liberty National for the privilege of working with you.

And thank you to Jon Finkel for helping me turn a lifetime of ups and downs and everything in between into the finished book you're holding today.

To the old crew—Eric Giglione, Mark Zipper, Larry Geneser, David Cohen, and Jim Surace: your camaraderie in those early years made it so much easier to get through the hard times.

Thank you to my Chicago crew—Sue Gilbert, Rona Spano, Mike Knapick, Scott Friedman, and Phil Bizare for following my lead as a sober SGA.

To Debbie Gamble, Diana Crosby, Ginny Castillo, Bo Gentile, Richard Meshulam, Durhon Oldham (my first director and later SGA of upstate New York), Scott Smith, Rob Falvo, Domenico Bertini, Larry Strong, and all the directors. Thank you for believing in my vision.

To some of my early Executive Council members: Bill Jennings, Tom Williams, and Theo Pappas. Your input helped change the course of AIL.

To the young guns—Marcus Smith, Simon Arias, Sabrina Lloyd, Zack and Mat Hart—who changed the whole demographic of AIL.

To Rick Altig and Ilija Orlovic for showing us what an American Income agency was actually capable of producing.

Thank you to the PR team—Denise Bowyer, Jules Pagano, Vic Kamber, Debbie Enstedt, Susan Fuldauer, Lori Pelletier, Laurie Onasch, Patti Morgan, Malka Arony, and Denise Gilbert—for your support of labor and our agency force.

To the Liberty Crew: Sally Fowler, Jason Everett, Brian Cannington, Sheri Young, Owen Wilson, Clint McLain, Tim Aderholt, Jeff Miller, Vickie Ketron, Angela Hanson, Roger Rich, Tin Nuckolls, and all the directors. Thank you for believing in us when nobody else did.

To the Torchmark (now Globe Life) crew: Joel Scarborough, Susan Allen, Frank Svoboda, Dolores Skarjune, and Vern Herbel. Thank you for understanding the nature of the beast.

To Larry Hutchison and Gary Coleman. Even though our cultures never meshed, thank you for believing in me and for being kind to me in my retirement.

To the great labor leaders that I have had the opportunity to learn from. John Sweeney, Rich Trumka, James Hoffa, Liz Schuler, Terry O'Sullivan, Morty Bahr, Sean McGarvey, Cecil Roberts, Chris Shelton, Lee Saunders, and many others.

Thank you so much for allowing me to see and understand the struggles that working families are going through, and for your dedication to creating positive change.

To my sister Tina, my brother Bob, my stepsisters Michele and Lori: I know you can't pick your family, but I sure am glad I ended up with you.

To my kids Nicole, Conrad, Emily, Adam, and Amiah: I love you all so much.

To my wife Demi: I will continue to try to be your hero.